Common threads

The Musical

Alex Pascall OBE

GRATEFUL ACKNOWLEDGMENTS

are made to the following:

Gwent Theatre in Education for commissioning me to write the original playscript; and the cast who first performed it to an audience of 12,000 in its three month run in South Wales; Gary Meredith, Chizzy Akudolu, Jain Boon, Daon Broni, Geddes Yates.

Acknowledgements are made to several people for their help;
To Milverton Wallace for his energy and commitment to see this project to its fruition; Ayandele Pascall; Sundance for his patience and understanding
Ingrid Wilson; Sharon Ford and Ken Davies of Big Pit (PWLL MAWR); Mining Museum (AMGUEDDFA LOFAOL) Blaenavon; Albert Mason; The management team of Tower Colliery; The Valley Inheritance Museum; Alfred Laws; Yvonne & Meurig Lewis; Phillip Yearwood; Barry Clayton; Roxy Harris; Rhondda Heritage Centre; Hirwaen Primary School; CADW; Welsh Historic Monuments; Roger Elsgood; Colin Bloxham; Harry Tootles Mining Dictionary; Rosie McCormick, Reed Educational & Professional Publishing Ltd; Desmond Johnson of Worldwide Inc PLC.

PICTURE CREDITS

Grateful acknowledgements are made to the following for the use of their photographs:

Photograph of Alex Pascall [p98] by Charles Green
(MASTER OF PHOTOGRAPHY)
Grenada Board of Tourism, Cardiff Council (Wales)
A.D.Tenzi, Jenny Barnes, Simon Rennie
Anthony Blake Photo Library
Illustrations of York House, Plantation House by W. Dieterle
Illustrations of Grenada Map; The Coal fields in South Wales – "Rock that burns", and Coal fields throughout the UK, by Joyce Rennie-Pascall

For further enquiries: Contact 0870 240 4698

LEYS FOR MILES WE'RE RISK
LL AND SHOVELS, AND DA

WE'RE RISKING OU
AND SHOVELS, AN
HEAT WITH GAS R

TRUCKING PONIE
DEAD BEAT

NY WAGE A WEEK
S FOR MILES WE'RE RISKING OU
SHOVELS, AND D
TH GAS RISING, RETREAT
G, PONIES WORKING! ALL SWE

ON THE FEET, REACH THE FAC
DEFEAT IT'S HARD
N. HANDS ARE ACHING, SORE

email: GVRM@email.com

First published in 2003 by Good Vibes Records and Music Limited
Registered Office: 1 Lamington Street, Hammersmith, London W6 0HU

First commissioned by Gwent Theatre in Education 2001

A catalogue record for this book is available from the Library of Congress, Washington D.C, USA.

British Library Cataloguing in Publication Data. A catalogue record for this book is available from the British Library, the University Library Cambridge, the National Library of Wales, Aberystwyth

ISBN 0-9517036-4-1

Printed and bound in UK by the Creative Print and Design Group
Originated in London

To Joyce — My Wife
whose words have been the inspiration to us all

"An idea is only worth its salt
when it blossoms into reality."

EDITORIAL STAFF

Editorial Director	Joyce Rennie-Pascall
Soundtrack Producer & Editorial Coordinator	Deirdre Pascall
Creative Director	Flora Awolaja
Editorial Adviser	Milverton Wallace
Typography, Layout & Cover Design	Blueparrotdesign
Photography Research	GVRM Photo Library Team

CONSULTANTS

Educational Consultants	Celia Burgess-Macey *Lecturer in Primary and Early Years Education, Goldsmiths College, University of London*
	Joan Goodie *Member of NATE – National Association for Teaching of English*
Assistant Editor Common Threads Q-Sheets	Kathy MacLean *Head of the Ethnic Minority Achievement – and Literacy Support Services. The Professional Centre for Teacher Training – Tooting Broadway, London*
Linguistic Terminology Consultant	Dr Morgan Dalphinis
Welsh Translator	Meg Ellis *Welsh Translators Society, Bangor University, North Wales*

CONTENTS

THE PLOT

In the 1950s, the sugar cane workers in Grenada and the miners in South Wales both felt they needed improvements in their working conditions. The injustices of the sugar cane barons' men of fortune, became increasingly unbearable, as planters' and miners' wages were minimally low, while the profits made from their toil were enormous.

Devine Cane, son of Papa Cane the planters' union leader, became the spokesman for the cane workers after his father's mysterious murder. The sugar cane workers would meet in secret places at night and at Shango ceremonies, often led by Mama Dlo, a spiritual guardian. The workers would discuss the demise of their plantation owner, Mr Warner, a wealthy baron and former highwayman. Warner had come from Wales to settle in Grenada and eventually owned plantations all over the Caribbean. He used the income from the sugar industry to develop coal mining and the iron ore industries in South Wales where he owned the coal mine, Big Pit Colliery.

Mama Dlo often gave speeches to the gathering of the cane field workers. Devine invites Mama Dlo to speak to his fellow workers to lift their spirits and lead them in prayer to deliver them from the evil of the fieldwork to a more prosperous future.

Phyllis, the goddaughter of Mama Dlo, was beautiful, and although she was admired by many, including Mr Warner for whom she worked as the housemaid at La Sagesse Estate, it was Devine, the tall and handsome son of Papa Cane, whom she loved. Some of the locals believed that she was a legendary Ladjablès, a stunning beauty who leads the disingenuous away to meet their uncertain end.

Phyllis tells Mama Dlo of the conversation she had overheard by the great house and that she is concerned for Devine's safety. She is aware of Mr Warner's interest in her, giving her special privileges in the household, in order to win her away from Devine. She says recently Mr Warner has shown himself to be wildly jealous and she expresses her fears as to the lengths he might go to destroy Devine, and begs Mama Dlo's guidance to make sure Devine too is not mysteriously murdered.

The night of Papa Cane's wake, held during the period of nine nights, is the last time Devine and Phyllis would see each other for decades to come. A flurry of spiritual rituals and rites are performed after the burial of Papa Cane, including the scheduled Shango, followed by prayers and psalms at Papa Cane's house. Family members, sugar cane growers and millers gather to celebrate his life in dance, song and storytelling, amidst traditional food delights, hot beverages, rum, and chants that create a magical atmosphere on a moonlit night. Devine is urged by Mama Dlo to flee the island on Captain Thomas Morgan's ship, the Sugar Queen, bound for the port of Cardiff. Devine is joined by his close friend Geddes, a tenor pan musician who is also keen to seek his fortune across the Atlantic.

Meanwhile, Mama Dlo has arranged for Phyllis to appear before Devine at St George's harbour dressed in her flowing white dress as a Ladjablès woman in all her splendour. She gives him a lump of charcoal, a totem, a good luck charm for his travels, aware that he will meet other members of the Wizzie Wizzie world who will recognise this symbol and take him in. Veiled in her disguise, she cannot reveal her true identity to Devine as she watches her lover leave the harbour, not knowing how many years will pass before she will see him again.

Once in Wales, the charcoal given to Devine plays its part in his fortunes and Hoof, King Sugar the donkey, informs us that South Wales, once pastoral in beauty, is now an industrial landscape covered in slag heaps brought about by coal mining.

Meanwhile, the wizard, Oz Mosis, active in wizzie circles globally, and also a union leader at Big Pit colliery, keeps in close contact with Mama Dlo through the wizzie, wizzie, web palm connection, generally known as the wwwpc, the wizzie world's latest communication tool. A device recessed within Oz and Mama Dlo's hands, it assists in the plans to bring Mr Warner to trial in an effort to obtain justice for his workers, their children and their children's children.

With Mama Dlo and Oz's plans for coordinated strike action in motion, the sugar cane workers cry "Sky Red!" to signal the burning of the cane fields of La Sagesse in Grenada, while simultaneously in South Wales, the colliers chant, "No Bonus, No Coal!" as they go on strike. Under the leadership of Oz and Devine, the strike continues until the miners meet face to face with Mr Warner at his trial held at the legendary Leaper's Hill *(Les Morne de Sauteurs)* in Grenada, where, by a web cast via the wwwpc, Warner comes face to face with the men, women and children he has oppressed and exploited over many years.

The trial is web cast, live to the workers of Big Pit, and eventually the secret of Warner's ill-gotten land, the root of his unhappiness and excessive drinking, is revealed. His fate is sealed, the workers condemn him and he is magically led under a spell to Leaper's Hill during the dance of Tuki, into the Wizzie Wizzie world of the Invisible, the place of wizards and sorceresses. There Warner can redeem himself.

Act 4 introduces the dawn of the 21st century, bringing with it big changes in the lives of the miners. At Tower Colliery, a new generation of miners now own a stake in their livelihood. Big Pit Colliery, which has been closed for many years, is now a mining museum. It is also a time for reunion and romance: the love unfulfilled between Devine and Phyllis in Grenada is reborn in the blossoming romance between their children Luci, Phyllis's daughter and Jazz the son of Devine. Devine and Phyllis are unexpectedly re-united, thanks to the magic of Mama Dlo and Oz Mosis, in their new guises as radio DJs. The marriage of Jazz and Luci symbolises the union of sugar and coal which still remains major energies influencing their lives in the new century.

THE WIZZIE WIZZIE WORLD OF THE INVISIBLE (WWWI)

Caribbean children of the 1950s lived in a creative and imaginary environment. Moonlight, and the canopy of stars added to the beauty of the night. Darkness confined the freedom of movement, but cultivated the mind's thirst for imagination. These were the moments when mythical characters like the Ladjablès, jumbies and other such mythical characters invaded the mind. The tree's shadows dancing in the moonlight across the windowpane formed images that fired the imagination. We made up stories to every movement and at times even imagined seeing some of those characters for real. It is this memory that gave birth to the Wizzie Wizzie World of the Invisible.

This is a fantastical world of imagination and cutting-edge technology, where we can fuse myth and reality to take stories into distant planets to arouse knowledge and deeper understanding of our world and its complexities.

The Wizzie Wizzie World of the Invisible is a fabulous realm populated with mythical characters, and also a haven for endangered species. It is located in the fathomless depths of a vast lake which is surrounded by a carpet of lush vegetation, fauna and flora. The air is scented with the aroma of rare fruits and spices.

Mama Dlo lives in a magnificent crystal palace deep beneath the lake. Her palace is guarded by ancient reptiles, the scariest of all being the five-headed cribo, whose body is covered with octopus-like tentacles. A large jewelled crown adorns each head. Mama Dlo is the Goddess of the Lake by decree of King Meteorolisis, the guardian of the magical universe of the invisible wizzie wizzie kingdom, whose extinction was threatened by the growth of greed and corruption from the world of reality. He comes to visit Mama Dlo once every thousand years, to consult on scientific advancement, futuristic activities and global disorder.

The Ancient Order of the Wizzie Wizzie. This is the oldest order of the Wizzie Wizzie World of the Invisible. Its ancient scripted charter defines the principles and governance of the WWWI.

The Comrades and Elders of The Wizzie Wizzie World. With the advent of advanced technology and global communication, Mama Dlo has decided to expand her forces by appointing Oz the wizard, leader of the miners, to monitor the western zone of workers and management, particularly in relation to environmental rehabilitation and workers' rights.

The Elders of The Wizzie Wizzie World. These are eminent scholars, men and women who are responsible for upholding the legal principles of the wizzie wizzie kingdom and the preservation of the animal domain, where new medicines and other scientific advancements are explored. From this comes the brew that transforms those found guilty of atrocities to prepare them for their rehabilitation in the Wizzie Wizzie World of the Invisible.
The three learned scholars, ***Asteroditis***, keeper of the heavenly bodies; ***Saccharoditus***, sage of

the sucrose kingdom; and ***Kinetisis,*** the master of all sources of energy, are all descendants of ***King Meteorolisis***, ruler of the cosmos.

The Motto of The Wizzie Wizzie World 'Non Palma Sin Labore' (No reward without labour), was translated from Hebrew into Latin by Saccharoditus.

Clarior-E-Tenebris ("Brighter out of darkness") is the insignia of excellence awarded to all who enter the WWWI believing in the dream that anything can be achieved. This was the saying of the ponies of long ago who journeyed in darkness through tunnels, valleys, and mountains and still knew how to lead suffering workers into the light and to new beginnings. It was first thought of as an insignia of hope for those who fell short of their civic duties and moral conduct and were able to overcome such weaknesses.

Tuki, one of the Carib women, who leapt from Leaper's Hill, is responsible for the preparation of the trial courts and the safe transport of those brought guilty to the Wizzie Wizzie World. She is ably assisted by Trotter, Hoof and others who meet the high qualities of her army.

The ***Doom Doom*** is the oldest drum in King Meteorilisis' Kingdom. It is used only on specific ceremonial occasions, or at the discretion of Mama Dlo and the three eminent scholars.

The ceremonial costumes of the representatives of the WWWI are a cultural spectacle to behold and the population of the WWWI always come out in vast numbers to attend the pageantry. At the request of the hard working, long serving donkeys and ponies, Mama Dlo and the Elders have decided to make the trial of Mr Warner a grand ceremonial occasion. This trial marks Oz's first appearance as a judge.

Wire bend, Wizzie end.

COMMON THREADS (CT) CHARACTERS

All the characters in this musical are fictitious

Trotter – A 20th century donkey, widely known as **King Sugar**. A Narrator playing the role of town crier. Member of the WWWI – **Grenada**

Devine Cane – A young coal activist who fled Grenada due to the murder of his father, Papa Cane, a sugar cane miller and mining activist – **Grenada & Wales**

Sagaboy – Sugar cane worker and activist – **Grenada**

Sousin (Sow sin) – Sugar cane worker – **Grenada**

Phyllis Duport – A dual personality – A beautiful Ladjablès and Devine's girlfriend. Phyllis is the mother of Luci Duport. – **Grenada**

Mr Glyn (Glin) **Warner** – Sugar estate owner and Coal baron – **Grenada/Wales**

Mama Dlo (Glow) – A Spiritual guardian from the Wizzie Wizzie World of the Invisible. The godmother of Phyllis Duport. A sorceress, a comrade of Oz Mosis. Her sole aim is to protect the Sugar cane workers and her goddaughter.

Oz Mosis – Ozwald Mosis - A dual personality – A wizard, born in Gwent and a trade union leader for the miners at Big Pit Colliery, South Wales. Also **DJ Oz** in act 4 – **Wales**

Adolphus Agree – La Sagesse Estate Overseer – **Grenada**

Capt Morgan Thomas Captain of a ship 'The Sugar Queen' – **Wales**

Geddes (Gédés) **Cool** – One of Devine's friends, a Steel pan musician who travels with Devine to South Wales and becomes a miner – **Grenada & Wales**

Father Fields – Roman Catholic Parish priest – **Grenada**

Tuki – One of the Carib women to leap from Leaper's Hill into the sea. This character is also a dancer, with responsibilities in the Wizzie Wizzie World of the Invisible.

Hoof – A 20th century pony widely known as **King Coal**. A Narrator playing the role of town crier. Member of the WWWI – **Wales**

Dafydd Ironpick – Coal Miner and union activist – **Wales**

Bossy – Chef for the miners' canteen – ***Wales***

Gweneira Mosis – Wife of Oz Mosis – ***Wales***

Jazz Cane – Son of Devine Cane, born and raised in Gwent, a senior mining archivist at Big Pit Museum – ***Wales***

Grazer – Son of Hoof with extrasensory powers of the Wizzie Wizzie World of the Invisible who has inherited his father's title of ***King Coal***. A Narrator playing the role of wedding reception toastmaster – ***Wales***.

Luci Duport – Daughter of Phyllis Duport, winner of St Lucia's island scholarship to study at the University of Cardiff, Wales to read Bio-technology – ***Wales***.

Meurig Cool – Son of Geddes Cool, Chairman of the new mining team – ***Wales***

Harry Ironpick – Son of Dafydd Ironpick, member of the new mining team for Tower Colliery – ***Wales***

DJ Oz – Oz Mosis in wizzie disguise – ***Wales***

DJ Wiz – Mama Dlo in wizzie disguise as an internet radio DJ – ***Grenada***

Bray – Son of Trotter, a 21st century donkey, with extrasensory powers of the Wizzie Wizzie World of the Invisible who has inherited his father's title of ***King Sugar***. A Narrator playing the role of wedding reception toastmaster – ***Grenada***

The 3 Scholars – of the WWWI – *Asteroditis*, keeper of the heavenly bodies; *Saccharoditus*, sage of the sucrose kingdom; and *Kinetisis*, master of all sources of energy

St Josephs Convent – Girls & Nuns Ensemble – A body of young school girls and Nuns

Growers and Millers' Ensemble – *Swing Ensemble Sugar cane Workers

Coal Miners' Ensemble – *Swing Ensemble Coal Miners

Common Threads Café Ensemble – *Swing clientele/customers inside Common Threads Internet Café

***Swing Ensemble:** Interchangeable characters. All actors/dancers can play the roles of both CT Ensemble, Coal Miners Ensemble and Growers and Millers Ensemble wherever possible.

ACTS & SCENES

Act 1

Act 2

Act 3

Act 4

"Wire bend, Wizzie end"

ACT ONE

SCENE :1

Suggestions on Characters, Text, Songs & Language.

In the beginning of this scene, Trotter & Hoof lead the audience in the traditional way of storytelling – Cric crac method, the call and response for permission to tell a story. [Hoof wears blinkers]

Older 'plantation' characters:
eg. Trotter & Mama Dlo predominantly speaks Creole

Characters in transition in age and class:
eg. Devine & Phyllis predominantly speaks mixed Creole/English

***(Line 41 col 4) Traditionally dominant character: eg. Mr Warner speaks Standard English*

Below:
Trotter

Cric Crac Trotter's Newsflash

Music: **The CT Prelude,**

Scene commences on the edge of the sugar cane field with La Sagesse sugar mill and millers in the distant twilight, near the estate owner's house overlooking the plantation where growers sharpen their cutlasses on a grinding stone while donkey carts wait to carry the sugar cane to the millers at the nearby mill at dawn.

Enter ***Growers and Millers Ensemble*** *along with* ***Trotter, Devine, Sagaboy,*** *and* ***Sousin*** *[Singing* ***Sweet Brown Sugar****] whilst* ***Growers and Millers*** *perform a dance sequence set in the cane field.*

Song: **Sweet Brown Sugar**

Enter ***Trotter*** *and* ***Hoof*** *[Wearing their respective donkey/pony headdress and costume]*

["Cric Crac" call and response is led by ***Trotter*** *on one side of the stage and* ***Hoof*** *on the other. They introduce the idea to the audience in a conversational and improvisatory style]*

Trotter	Cric
Audience	Crac
Hoof	Cric
Audience	Crac
Trotter	Sugar
Audience	Sugar
Hoof	Coal
Audience	Coal,
Trotter	Sugar, sugar, sugar
Hoof	Coal, coal, coal
Trotter	Sugar, sweet, sugar
Hoof	Coal, carbon, coal

*[****Ensemble*** *continue action only during* ***Trotter's*** *monologue]*
*[****Trotter*** *ends the audience participation ad lib before launching into narration and acts of wizardry while making the sound of a mountain-dove]*

Trotter

Imagine dawn on the island of Grenada in the Caribbean with the incessant crowing of the cockerels, the braying of donkeys, birds singing, footsteps and distant voices in the cool morning breeze.

The sugar cane workers of La Sagesse estate in the Parish of St David are gathering to begin the day's cane cutting. It's only two weeks to the end of the crop-over season. Life bubbles in the heat of the sun in different directions. It's life between happiness and uncertain financial expectations. 'Tween rivalry and revelry, love and hate, production and counter production, sorcery and energy. It's a difficult time for the workers in their dealings with a certain gentleman of fortune, the greedy plantation owner, Mr Warner.

The air is a thick cloud of growing anger as Papa Cane, the founder and head of La Sagesse trade union is mysteriously killed. The workers set fire to one of Mr Warner's outhouses amid cries of Sky Red. For many planters and sugar mill workers it is Mr Warner who seems responsible. His wages are low, just one meagre dollar a day working from dawn till dusk with promises to raise the pay consistently and conveniently ignored. With men, women and children toiling to produce sweet brown sugar under the rays of the hot sun, any worker who questions the boss's authority faces immediate sacking.

SCENE :2

Scene: ***Unrest on the sugar cane fields of La Sagesse Estate***

Music: ***Sweet Brown Sugar*** *Interlude*

Enter three workers from the cane fields and ***Mama Dlo*** *working.* ***Sousin, Adolphus Agree,*** *and* ***Sagaboy*** *[centre stage]* ***Mama Dlo,*** *spiritual leader and secretly a sorceress, prepares lunch for the workers, over a* ***coal-pot fire****.*

Trotter

Over there, Mama Dlo is sitting; peeling sweet potatoes, yams and making dumplins. The pot is already on the boil in preparation for the workers' lunch. Over there, the workers are cutting sugar cane; they gather and tie bundles together, heaped by the roadside. Here I stand, my cart ready and waiting to be loaded for transporting the sugar cane to the main road for the trucks which will take the cane to the factory for grinding. "Time means production, production equals profits". The plantation owner Mr Warner is profit mad, ***look him deh***, looking out he ***jalousie*** window! But, here comes Devine with my load.

Devine

[Calling to everyone]
[Walking down towards ***Mama Dlo*** *from the front of the estate house]*

All you hurry, let's move fast, we must meet around lunchtime, enough is enough, this mongoose man Warner think we stupid. He want us to load the trucks *[walks in* ***Trotter's*** *direction]* finish cutting all the three acres of sugar cane before he will decide whether or not we are eligible for a bonus. This man mad! You ain't hear? He fire Johnny from the mill. I guess he think the sugar will boil itself!

All

[chanting] No Bonus, No Crop!
No Bonus, No Crop!

Sagaboy

Words! Eh eh, I know, that's all he has to offer, that crab Warner. Tell he to take he cutlass and come and cut the cane himself, that petticoat drunkard! He like an iguana, ***a real man pattern***, he think he playing with school children. Is fire he playing with! He better watch it. ***Ah sure*** he made his money like a highwayman stealing abroad. He think he have book sense and we have ***crab mentality***? Well, well, that ***book a dull,*** I could read he like a book, I could ***read he upside down***.
[Laughing, ***Steups*** *– sucks his teeth]*

Sousin

I goin' get Mama Dlo to fix he up properly with a good ***Cou Cou soup***. Tell that man don't play with trouble. I already have enough of my own, but if he really want trouble, I could land him some easy.
[She spits in disgust]
Mama Dlo will help fix him. We believe that she know witchcraft in truth and they say she goddaughter Phyllis is a ***Ladjablès*** too.

Sagaboy

[speaking under his breath]
I wonder if Devine knows and if so, why hasn't she fixed Mr Warner yet? Maybe she's biding time.

Enter ***Mr Warner*** *[passing through - speaking to* ***Mama Dlo****]*

****Mr Warner**

Get a move on, what going on here? What's all this about a meeting? The only meeting is to finish cutting all the cane! Stop ***scratching zouti and smelling about***. What you sow, that you'll reap, bonus may come later. Get a move on!

***Above**: Sousin and Mama Dlo talking.*

Suggestions on Characters, Text, Songs & Language.

***(Line 13 col 1) Shango – A ceremony led by Mama Dlo, performed by the Yoruba tribe of Africa for the Goddess of Thunder. This ceremony is popular throughout the Southern Caribbean and held so that the gods would send rain to replenish the crops and heal the infirm.*

(Line 22 col 1)* ***Creole/French (cf.)
*****Wavet pa ni wezon douvan poul***
[The cockroach has no rights in front of the chicken]

Useful Resource: *Dictionary of Caribbean English Usage by* ***Richard Allsopp****, Oxford University Press, 1996*

Mama Dlo

*[Out of **Warner's** earshot, whilst he is walking around looking at the workers]*

Put pyjamas on monkey, monkey believe he become man! ***Give a goat an inch a slack it goin' take a foot!***

*[She lifts her dress discreetly to reveal her one cow foot, without **Mr Warner** observing, for the audience to see]*

Ha, ha, ha! Poor fool, ***she who holds the iron knows the heat***. By the way, Sousin girl, how are things getting on? I hope you coming to the ***** Shango*** tonight?

Sousin

Sure Mama Dlo, cause I want my kids to stop working in the hot sun and go to school so they can open their brain and learn. It's the only way to make headway. I hear you say di cockroach we want to ***ketch*** parading again. *****Wavet pa ni wezon douvan poul***.

[Laughter from all]

*[All workers sing 2nd verse and chorus of **Sweet Brown Sugar** as they go back to work]*

*Enter **Adolphus Agree***

Agree

Break it up, break it up, Sousin! Morning Mama Dlo, how things today? Come on, come on you lot, move it up.

Mama Dlo

Things are just the same way your boss left it two days ago.
life on this plantation ***full up ah things and things***.

Agree

How do you mean?

Mama Dlo

Ah ah, can't you see for yourself? A man of your standing must have a little more than common sense! Just look! Johnny have no job since you helped sack him, he children need food to eat like all ah we and by the way, the workers all saying is you responsible for the death of we union leader Papa Cane. Just look at the workers, nobody happy any more. No medical facilities - this place used to be alive, even with Mr Warner bad ways and ***maga*** wages. Now ***crapaud*** and all gone silent; ***still water does run deep***. You think you and Mr Warner could do as you like and he get away with it? You must be mad! What goes up must come down.

*[**Mr Warner** walks towards **Devine** who is cutting cane]*
[Workers looking on anxiously]

Warner

Devine, you, Devine; I understand you are planning a union meeting today? Are you out of your senses?

Devine

You seem to have extrasensory hearing.
[Keeps on working]

Sagaboy

*[To **Devine**]*

This man looking for ruin. Ignore he man!

Warner

Let's get this quite straight; there is just one boss on this estate, that's me, Warner! There is no room for the likes of you and your trade union nonsense! Cut out this stupid agitation and get on with it! I expect to hear nothing more, or else!

Devine

Or else, or else! Come let me give you 'or else'.

Sousin

*[Singing out of earshot of **Mr Warner**]*

Shu fly don't bother me, shu fly don't bother me, go and find you own company.

Sagaboy

Excuse me Mr Warner?

*[Moves towards **Mr Warner** to have a quiet word, walking away from **Devine**]*

But Mr Warner, you ***crampin me style***, I don't know the last time ah manage to buy new clothes. ***All ah we*** under pressure, we grinding day and night. When the day is done, I like to get dressed and ***lime*** along the ***Carenage*** round we beautiful horseshoe-shaped harbour.

I like to ***look sharp*** to chat up the ladies, I mean I trying hard to find a nice wife.

*[He smiles at **Sousin**]*

I don't know when last I see Mr John to be fitted for a new trousers. Four weeks now he waiting for me, cause he have new material from the US and England. ***I done see*** the film with me trousers in it. The best materials any tailor can provide. But you think I could get pay? I don't know the last time ah buy a new trousers. Mr Warner you ***crampin me style!*** Respect yourself man, ***listen to we***, cause since you take over, La Sagesse affairs are a disgrace in the planting business.
Yes Mr Warner, they say, "Cain killed Abel", but I goin' to make sure cutting sugar cane for you don't kill me!

Sousin

[whispering]

Cool it Sagaboy and you Devine, he ***cou cou*** burn already. We goin' deal with that mongoose Warner, just look at he! He like a ghost, he a ***jumbie***.

*[In **Warner's** direction]*

Alé! Alé man! Hence, Satan, hence, you full ah ***bagasse***, ***always in we tail!***

*[**Steups**. Leads chanting of **Go Mr Warner**]*

*Song: **Go Mr Warner***

*[**Warner** walks away towards the estate house. **Devine** is furious; the workers calm him down]*

Sagaboy

Devine, we don't want you to end up like ***ya*** father, Papa Cane. Can't you see that man ***just baiting*** for you? Worst of all, he hate the fact that Phyllis is so deeply in love with you. Warner think every beautiful woman who works on this plantation is part of he estate belongings. That man ***too fresh up*** with himself.

Sousin

What you and Phyllis have to do is to get yourselves away from this estate. That man Warner have his eye on her, but she could yet be the one to fix his business.

Devine

What! Eye on my girlfriend? He ***full ah*** rubbish…I done warn Phyllis about cockroaches like he already, he better don't play he freshness.

Mama Dlo

I watching him like nobody business. I goin' bait him like a ***crayfish***. That man don't just like woman, he love sweet food too and good ***rum***, and as the saying goes, ***'sweet food kill cow'. I throw me corn me no call no fowl***.

Devine

The day he touch my Phyllis, he will cease to be Mr Warner. He like a ***rum shop jumbie*** only sipping rum ***fe his mischief***. ***Crapaud smoke he pipe.***

*[Laughter from **Sagaboy**]*

*[**Devine** leads **Go Mr Warner** chant]*

notes

Suggestions on Characters, Text, Songs & Language.

*****Props and settings** *[Scene 3] Fireplace with a coal pot on it, a log box, chess set with CT characters eg King Coal & King Sugar, a rum barrel, long stick of sugar cane [as a ladle for stirring the pot], Davey lamps, miner's hard hat and other wizzie artifacts.*

The palm of Oz's hand, known throughout the drama as the ***wwwpc,*** *contains a device that is powered by heat which causes the palm to glow and enables Oz Mosis and Mama Dlo to communicate and see each other via web casts and view picture and video or DVD footage.*

Below: *A coal miners Davey Lamp*

Mama Dlo

Well, the meeting go happen anyway, all you coming? I see you tonight at eight when work done and after I see Phyllis. Don' forget to bring the chicken for the Shango, we get the goat already. See you later! Watch how you go, take it easy.

*[**Mama Dlo** leaves to go into the Estate house to see **Phyllis**]*

**SCENE :3

In the tower of Big Pit Wizzie Wizzie Brew

Music: ***Coal Miner's Waltz***
[Underscore for ***Big Pit Colliery*** *scenes]*

Scene: ***Miners at work in Big Pit Colliery*** *– full production sequence. At the end of it,* ***Oz Mosis*** *can be seen climbing to the tower. The tower is* ***Oz's*** *thinking tower/office. A masterfully designed secret office - complete with a fireplace, coal fire burning, a pot, a log box, photos of his mining crew, a Davey lamp, machinery, and large chess set, a rum casket as his treasure chest. He uses a long stick of sugar cane as a ladle for stirring the barrel, as his wizzie thinking/plotting tool and other items etc.* ***Oz*** *stops occasionally in between his monologue to engage the audience in call and response ideas, using some of the lines in his delivery to get them to interact while blending his wizzie brew stew.*

*[**Hoof** blows a* ***conch shell*** *as a welcome for* ***Oz****]*

Enter ***Oz Mosis***
[Stirring his barrel of wizzie wizzie brew]
*[**Oz** is in the winding tower of Big Pit in his wizzie office in conversation with himself it seems]*

Oz Mosis

Remember me, later I may appear before you cloaked in guises as I dare to help navigate this web of common threads, with the help of other wizzie wizzie friends. Surely you know me....

[He looks into the wizzie wizzie barrel and then towards his imaginary audience]

Surely you know that I'm really a wizard, maybe it's a wizzie thing, people just don't understand. So, just to ***spice things up*** a bit – ***to boot!*** I've got a split personality. My wizard comrades call me Oz, the Wizard, but here in Wales I'm Oz Mosis, the **Miners' Union** leader, just an ***amoebic*** guise, to help the miners free their minds and release some of the shackles of mining coal. Don't mind me, I'm just here to stir a little wizzie wizzie wizzie, coal coal coal, sugar sugar sugar, coal coal coal.

[Adds what looks like Common Thread characters and other ingredients to the wizzie wizzie brew]

Maybe you *[steals a glance at the audience]* can help me add to this recipe in time....where common threads, two worlds and energies collide.

[Mumbles the names of some characters as each effigy plops into the barrel of wizzie wizzie brew]

We'll ***just sit tight*** and watch! 'Cos many eyes keep the pot bubbling like brown sugar and crackling like coal! In a room filled with energies, stories unfold!

Music: ***Wizzie Wizzie Wizzie***
Instrumental Interlude

*[**Oz** invites audience to repeat
each phrase]*

Sugar, sugar, sugar,
crackle, crackle fireflies crackle!

Sugar, sugar, sugar,
crackle, crackle fireflies crackle!

Sugar, sugar, sugar,
crackle, crackle fireflies fly

Cribo crawls, fowl sleep,
owl peep at Ladjablès feet,
[Laughter]

Crapaud call *[**Oz** imitates the noises
of a frog, giggles, then raps the **Wizzie
wizzie wizzie** rap]*

Song: ***Wizzie Wizzie Wizzie***

CHORUS 1
**Do the wizzie wizzie wizzie brew
Do the wizzie wizzie wizzie stew
Wizzie wizzie wizzie
Wizzie wizzie wizzie
Wizzie wizzie, wizzie wizzie
Wizzie wizzie wizzie**

**Brew brew wizzie wizzie brew
Stew stew wizzie wizzie stew
Do the Wizzie wizzie wizzie
wizzie wizzie wizzie
Wizzie wizzie wizzie wizzie
wizzie wizzie wizzie**

**Glow glow coal glow
Bubble bubble molasses bubble
Do the wizzie wizzie wizzie brew
Do the wizzie wizzie wizzie stew
Coal coal coal digging in de hole
Fire fire fire coal pot fire
Burn fire burn canefield burn
Sky red!**

CHORUS 2
**Wizzie Wizzie brew
Wizzie wizzie stew
Wizzie
Wizzie wizzie wizzie wizzie brew**

**Bubble bubble toil and trouble
Fire burn and cauldron bubble
Do the wizzie wizzie wizzie brew
Do the wizzie wizzie wizzie stew
Stew stew what mirrors you
Something borrowed or
something new
Something old or something blue
Just follow me 'cause it's all
in the stew**

(REPEAT CHORUS 2)

**Crackle crackle fireflies crackle
Cribo crawls while fowls sleep
Owls peep at Ladjablès feet
Whey horse reach donkey
must reach**

**They say whey horse reach donkey
must reach
What mirrors time triggers
the mind
Ask no questions tell no lies
Set no molasses catch no flies
Set no molasses catch no flies**

(REPEAT CHORUS 1)

**It's a tale of mystery
Web palms history
Do the wizzie wizzie wizzie brew
Do the wizzie wizzie wizzie stew
Coal and rum A yarn of myth
Wizzie wizzie wit No hit and miss
Water stand up Water lie down
What goes up surely must
come down**

CHORUS 2
Wizzie Wizzie brew

notes

Wizzie wizzie stew
Wizzie
Wizzie wizzie wizzie wizzie brew

No you do dis and I do dat
No Tit for tat butter for fat
Just justice
No you do dis and I do dat
No Tit for tat butter for fat
Just justice

CHORUS 2
Wizzie Wizzie brew
Wizzie wizzie stew
Wizzie
Wizzie wizzie wizzie wizzie brew

*[**Wizzie wizzie wizzie** song fades out]*

Oz Mosis
[Tossing a piece of coal into the air]
Toils for love, coal to light.

[Light appears SFX - neighing of a pit pony]

*[**Oz** talks to himself as he continues to stir the Wizzie wizzie stew]*

Bubble, bubble, bubble, molasses bubble
Sugar cane make sweet sweet
brown sugar.
Make Rum! Make Candy!
Money! Sugar right?
Ha, ha! Ha, wizzie, wizzie funny!
Ask no questions tell no lies
Set no molasses catch no flies.

[Licking his lips pretending to chase a fly]
Shu shu, Shu shu
Brew brew, wizzie wizzie brew
Stew stew, what mirrors coal for you?
Murder for him, love for her.
Between sugar and coal! Watch it sir.

[Grumbling]
Run, run mongoose out of town
Dog coming run for your life

Life of sugar, life of coal. Strike strike!
None must stroll. Common threads all
play a role! Behold, what goes up, must
come down. ***Monkeys say cool breeze, Crapaud says wait until tomorrow***.

Riches for one, riches for all.
What mirrors sugar mirrors you
Brew brew, wizzie, wizzie brew
Stew, stew, wizzie, wizzie stew

What mirrors time triggers the mind
Coal loves pony, sugar loves donkey!
They say **whey horse and pony reach donkey must reach**.
Donkey, take your time but do it fast.

[Pigeon SFX]
Coo Coo, Coo Coo, Coo coo.

Something borrowed, something new?
Something old? Love never grows cold!

Bubble, bubble toil and trouble
Fire burn and cauldron bubble
Brew, brew wizzie, wizzie brew
Stew, stew wizzie, wizzie stew
Pot boil, sugar boil, burn fire burn
Burn fire, fire burn! Set molasses, stew…
Coo Coo, Coo Coo, Coo Coo
Coo Coo, Coo Coo, Coo Coo

*[**Oz's** barrel and Wizzie wizzie brew must mysteriously disappear]*

SCENE :4

Household duties at
La Sagesse Estate

*Music: **Sweet Brown Sugar** Interlude*

*Scene: **Mama Dlo** meets with **Phyllis** inside La Sagesse Estate. **Phyllis** is seen making up **Mr Warner's** bed late morning, weeping.*

Below: *Plantation estate house*

*Enter **Mama Dlo** calling **Phyllis***

Mama Dlo

Phyllis, Phyllis, is your godmother, where are you? Phyllis, what's wrong, come on child tell me, who upset you, who? Devine?

*[**Phyllis** burst into tears and falls into **Mama Dlo's** arms]*

Phyllis

No! No! It's not poor Devine! I just don't know what to do, but we have to do something quick Mama Dlo. I don't want to lose him, I love Devine. Mama Dlo please don't let them kill him too. Don't stay Mama Dlo, move quick before Mr Warner get back any minute now and see you.

Mama Dlo

Kill Devine? Lord, child, this place will go up in smoke! One death is enough! We won't let him meet the same fate as he father. OK? Brace yo'rself girl, don't let Warner catch you crying. We goin' to arrange for the Shango to happen tonight. Before Papa Cane **wake**. Don' fret child. I'll see you later.

*[**Phyllis** looks out of the bedroom window and sees that **Mr Warner** is now walking towards the estate, with a bottle of rum and a sugar cane stick]*

Phyllis

Mama Dlo, pass in the back, I could see Warner coming up the pathway. Ah go walk through the cane field, he wouldn't be sober enough to tell who it is.

*[**Phyllis** leaves the estate singing **Sweet Brown Sugar** acappella]*

*[**Phyllis** passes by **Mr Warner** disguised as a Ladjablès]*

Phyllis

Morning Glyn, *[she looks at him from head to foot]* look at your state! You like a **dotish** crayfish out of water, but I can fix that. You can tell me your secrets anytime OK? Just look for me down at the harbour.

Mr Warner

What a darling! Do I know you? Come hold my hand! I need some sugar to sweeten my life, ha! ha! You look quite beautiful in your white dress.

*[**Warner** begins to sing]*

Song: ***Show me the way to go home***
[Sung acappella]

Show me the way to go home
I'm tired and I want to go to bed
I had a little drink about an hour ago
And it's gone right to my head
[Laughs]

No matter where I roam
On land or sea or foam
You will always hear me singing
my song
Show me the way to go home

*[**Warner** walks away slowly staggering his way to the house, as **Mama Dlo** passes **Mr Warner** on her way to serve lunch to the **Growers** and **Millers**]*

Mama Dlo

*[Speaks under her breath in close proximity to **Warner**]*

Look at the cockroach, any fowl could swallow he now, you think you' the only hot rooster in this farmyard!

*[speaks directly to **Warner**]*
Eh? How come ***you like cow and you have no respect for its calf?*** You are a

notes

Suggestions on Characters, Text, Songs & Language.

*** *(Line 18 col 4) Traditionally dominant characters in Eastern Caribbean countries eg.* ***Father Fields*** *speaks Standard English.*

Below: *Sugar cane fields being harvested*

real iguana, what a disgrace to humankind. Get it straight man, if you ***trouble trouble, then trouble bound to trouble you***. I'll tell you who is we king on this plantation, is ***we donkey***, Trotter. Without he carrying the load out to de lorries, cane will never reach de factory.

Our Trotter, he got more common sense than all like you and he, poor ***jackass,*** is we king. Jackass! You can't even stand up to save your life, but you chasing me goddaughter and you a murderer, watch out. ***What ain't pass you don't say it miss you.***

*[**Warner** walks toward the house]*

*Exit **Mama Dlo***
[She heads back towards the fields to begin serving lunch]

*Enter **Adolphus Agree***

Mama Dlo

Good day, Mr Adolphus Agree. You not on duty just now! You not Mr Overseer right now! I notice the likes of you who were lying low, playing Little Bo Peep *[clears her throat]* know just when to appear for nourishment.

*[**Agree** gives her a stay quiet, don't aggravate the situation, look]*
Who the cap fit let them wear it.
[Laughter and chatter among all the workers awaiting their meal]

*Enter **Devine** [singing]*

Go Mr Warner got to go,
he got to go, he got to go.

*[**Sousin** dancing and taunting **Agree**]*

Sousin

*[singing **Sweet Brown Sugar's** chorus, acappella]*

Sugar, sugar, sugar, sugar cane…

Ah! Ah! Agree boy is that you, what happening? The food smell bring you out in the open, it's good to see you man.

Agree

Mama, you' dumplins looking delicious. I favour some of that delicious salt-beef; treat me right. *[looking at **Sousin**]* Mama Dlo know I nice.

Sousin

Yes, nice to ketch anybody who touch we leader Devine.

Mama Dlo

Agree you know what Papa Cane used to say before they kill him? He say we must never forget that ***what look nice from far is often far from nice!*** Get what I mean? ***Calabash*** always pretty outside, but inside always rotting. ***Ketch*** yourself, you think you nice!

Agree

All you ease up nah! I just easy, all you should know me well, I like a blade of sugar cane, ah ***cutting on both sides***. Overseer must always agree not to disagree and love everybody. I neutral. It's OK, I in a good mood, as long as I get some of you' delicious soup and my share of dumplins!

Mama Dlo

Agree! Take you' food quick then eat and just take your exit. Keep out of the way cause if you ***rush de brush you'll get daub!*** Don't push you' luck.

Sagaboy *[singing]*

We till the soil, grow the crop
sugar cane
Machete, Man, Woman, Child
cutting sugar cane
For little money, that's not funny
trucking cane

Juicy, juicy, juicy, juicy sugar cane

[Exit]

SCENE :5

Inside La Sagesse

Early evening, inside La Sagesse, ***Mr Warner*** *in the dining room, with a decanter of rum on the table near an oak chest.*

Scene: ***Warner Accounting***

Mr Warner
Phyllis! Phyllis, bring me some water.
Hurry, hurry.

Phyllis
Is that all you need sir? *[Whispering]*
One smell of alcohol and the big man
is just like a **cockroach in front frizzle fowl**. Man like he think because he big he large. One day he goin' get what Polly give the drum; it's called blows.

Mr Warner
Just water to begin! *[Lying!]*
And another glass.

Phyllis
[Under her breath]
Yes, water. **'Blood thicker than water, but his thin with rum'**. Money pouring out of this man's ears, but the workers can't get a penny raise of pay. What a greedy thief, and if he' not careful, all the sugar cane will stay right there and sour, and the factory will just stop work.
Long rope for magga goat.
He **penny wise and pound foolish**.

Phyllis
Would you like some **guava cheese**
with you' water sir?

Mr Warner
How sweet. Too much sugar and cane
for the day. Water will do.

Phyllis
[Serves ***Mr Warner*** *his drink in a hurry]*
Sir, sir! Mr Warner, Mr Warner!
Father Fields is approaching the estate.

Mr Warner
Good Lord Phyllis, clean up this mess and take these bottles to the refiner. Leave the glasses and I'll keep a bottle just in case. I'll send word that I've sampled the new stock and it's fit for drinking.
My good friend is at the door.

****Father Fields**
[Shouting] Is anyone home?
Hello! Hello! Mr Warner, Phyllis are you in, it's Father Fields?

Phyllis
[Hurries to the door]
Hello Father, please come in. I was busy in the kitchen and I've just made some **guava cheese**. Would you like some?

Father Fields
Oh! My favourite. Bless you Phyllis, it smells delicious, you are so industrious.
Thank you. It's good to see you.
What a beautiful person you are.
God bless you my child.

*[****Father Fields*** *notices* ***Mr Warner*** *trying to rise from the table]*

Don't get up man, conserve your energy. What are you doing to yourself old boy? You look........

Mr Warner
[Looking cunningly at ***Father Fields****]*
Looks can be deceiving.

*[****Father Fields*** *sniffs the air loudly]*

notes

I was just breezing out, taking in the fragrant sugar cane breeze.
[Glances at the spilt glass of rum]

Phyllis! Phyllis What's all this water under the table? Will you bring some cloth to wipe it up.

Phyllis
Yes, sir.

Mr Warner
This house is blessed with the best spirits Father *[clears his throat]* Phyllis, please bring Father a glass. We must make a toast to our absent friends.

Father Fields
Well said Glyn. May the Lord bless our sugar cane and yield for us a fruitful harvest. May La Sagesse overflow and provide bountiously for the meek and needy.

*[**Mr Warner** and **Father Fields** raise their glasses]*

Mr Warner
First for the day. God knows how much I need it. Let's ***wet our whistle*** then shall we? Bottoms up!

Father Fields
Glyn Warner, you are such a lucky man, you have such a faithful bunch of workers, you don't even have the problems the other estates are having. You are so Lucky!

Mr Warner
You know Father, in life, the cattle that's silent in the sun is often weaker than the one making all the noise. The silent one is always too weak to call for water. Now Phyllis is so good to me, that no one would ever know my weaknesses.

Below: Phyllis serving whilst Mr Warner is doing his accounts.

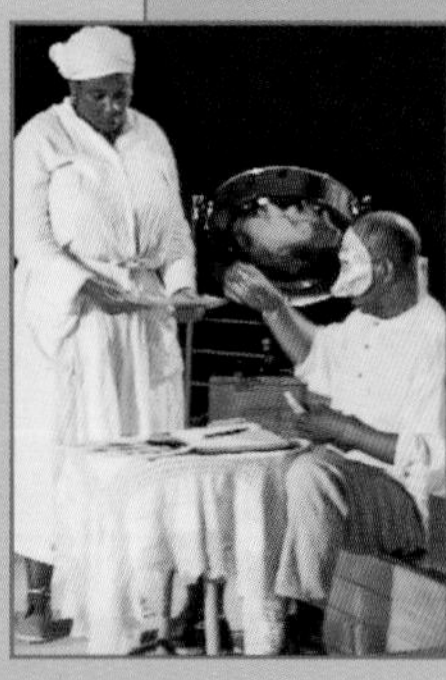

Father Fields
Bless her! I've not seen you since the night of Papa Cane's untimely end, and we have not seen you at mass for sometime, neither have you come for confession lately. You are becoming a hermit, man! We cannot allow that to happen to you. Are you feeling OK? Your presence in church and your voice in the choir means so much to the other parishioners.

Mr Warner
You know Father, this ***crop over*** harvesting time is always the busiest period, and this one is no exception. It is proving very difficult. The workers are very uncooperative. This new wave of trade unionism is becoming a scourge to my estate here, and back home in Wales I am facing union revolt. And since Papa Cane aroused these workers, now led by his son Devine, they are putting up all manner of demands. Father, they'll have me in ruin if I let them.

Phyllis
Father, a pot of tea, guava cheese and some fruit cake.

Father Fields
Yes, my child. By the way Phyllis, when will Devine and yourself come and see me about exchanging your vows? You are such a lovely couple, that is all Papa Cane used to pray for.

Phyllis
Our marriage Father?

Mr Warner
Talk is cheap. Here in Grenada they say, ***If all wishes were horses all beggars would ride***. I have made it quite clear to Phyllis that if she marries Devine he would no longer be tolerated anywhere on this estate. She is well looked after here by me and

that is as far as it goes. The buck stops here.

*[**Phyllis** pours out a cup of tea and serves cake to **Father Fields** in dead silence, then leaves the room]*

Father Fields

Why pour oil on already troubled waters man? Are you ready to dig your own grave and bury yourself? Mama Dlo came to see me recently, very worried she is, and so upset at the way you are treating Phyllis. As a friend Glyn, I don't mind telling you, you will make the worst mistake of your life trying to separate Phyllis from Devine. Especially now that Papa Cane is dead and gone. Lord help the one responsible for his mysterious death. He was the heart of the workers and you were both pillars of strength in the church.

Phyllis

Sir?

Mr Warner

Yes, Phyllis.

Phyllis

Did you tell Father about the dream you had about the river overflowing and **dirty water** running through the house?

Mr Warner

Father is too busy to listen to all this mumbo jumbo nonsense.

Father Fields

I must not overstay my visit. I have to go to prepare for confessions. I am most pleased to have seen you, Glyn.

Mr Warner

Your visits mean so much to me. You are the only one, apart from Phyllis, who cheers me up.

Father Fields

You know friendship is the most precious gift. It affords me the additional energy to look after my flock. My parishioners are like a rich harvest, and without the blessing of the rain to bring forth the harvest we will all perish for thirst. The workers would lose faith and energy, and our wonderful world would be a sad and lonely place to live. Man, as captains, we must always heed the tides. Be of good spirits!

Mr Warner

A last one for the road Father?

Father Fields

Oh no! One is more than enough. A bite is as good as a feast.

Mr Warner

Well, cheers, I'll drink for us both. Phyllis! Please see Father Fields to the door.

Phyllis

Father, I've prepared the guava cheese for you to take with you. *[Takes him to the door]*

Mr Warner

[Grumbling]

Getting married, exchanging vows? Over my dead body! He who pays the piper, calls the tune. I am the boss, they'll dance to my command. Listen, Phyllis! Phyllis!

*[**Phyllis** appears]*

Go to your godmother! *[pause]* Tell her to come and see me with Devine. I want to make them a personal offer, one they can't refuse. As long as they stop this silly union nonsense, I will give them a bonus, but not the rest of the workers. You heard me.

Phyllis

Yes, Mr Warner. *[under her breath]* ***Monkey say cool breeze, Crapaud say wait until tomorrow***. What a **mouth champion**

*[**Phyllis** leaves, crosses **Aldolphus Agree** at the door]*

SCENE:6

Mama Dlo's plan

*Scene: Late evening, the rain is falling heavily as **Phyllis** arrives at **Mama Dlo's** house near the sugar mill.*

[SFX - Barking of dogs and night atmosphere]

Phyllis

[Knocking]

Mama Dlo! Is me, Phyllis!

Mama Dlo

I know it's you! I can see your little cow foot. You practising walking in the dark without a long dress! Girl, as soon as darkness come, from now on when you are outside you have to cover up your foot. Ladjablès can't let people find out this other side of their **wizzie** personality. They done talking already of your beauty. This charm will be the downfall of all those fresh up men like Warner; we will get rid of them, one by one. Soon I'll take you to Leaper's Hill. That's **whey** all di bad and covetous men does vanish since the days of the ***Caribs***. Not one can escape.

Phyllis

Have you seen Devine, Mama Dlo?

Mama Dlo

Yes, I know where he is! I am taking full care to ensure that he gets out of Grenada. Sorry, Phyllis, but unless I do that, he will become a corpse. I can't let him face what he father, Papa Cane, met. Trust me, I'll deliver him to safe hands. OK?

Phyllis

Mama No!

Mama Dlo

Yes. Girl brace yourself! As soon as he goes we will fix Warner! I will make contact with Oz, he's a wizard in South Wales, one of us; in time you will meet. On your way back, tell Sousin to gather the people and arrange the Shango. Come to the Shango. This is Ladjablès time, cover your feet girl, make sure you well disguise and be by the ship 'Sugar Queen' to see when Devine is leaving. Take this bit of charcoal, wrap it up and just give it to him as he's passing to board the ship. This will assure his arrival in Wales. Phyllis, the coal in Wales isn't the same as charcoal, but they have something in common.

Make haste, then meet me back at the Shango. I'm on my way. I go have plenty to say tonight.

SCENE :7

Shango and Papa Cane's wake

Trotter

It's Nine Nights, after the burial of Papa Cane, a celebration of his life. Tonight, spiritual guardian, Mama Dlo, speaks to the millers and planters to raise their spirits and lead them in prayer to deliver their minds from evils and

Suggestions on Characters, Text, Songs & Language.

***(Line 2 col 3) For this ceremony **Mama Dlo** is dressed in the traditional red and white colours of the shango, the god of thunder and lightning. She sprinkles water ceremonially to purify the ground and the participants.*

***(Line 13 col 3) **Shango** – [The people are all dressed in red and white clothes. All are barefooted. The ritual involves a chicken as part of the ceremony]*

***Below:** An Orisha drum used for the Shango dance*

hardships into tranquil waters. Devine was accustomed to inviting **Mama Dlo to speak to them and lead them in a prayer before performing the Shango ceremony. I'm just trotting by to put my ears to good use and pay my respects to we late Papa Cane.

Song: ***Shango Mama Dlo***

*[Dance sequence depicting the **Shango ceremony]*

***Phyllis** and **Devine** sit talking on the veranda of Papa Cane's house while Psalm 23 is being hummed from inside*

Agree

Tonight we gather here to celebrate the life of our Papa Cane to pray that the lord will have mercy on his soul and welcome him to eternal life.

Growers and Millers Ensemble

Amen.

Sousin

Amen. Praise the lord.

Agree

May his soul rest in peace. Let us do the Hail Mary and the Lord's Prayer, to get to the eating.

Sagaboy

[Singing]

Bring it Mr Chairman, bring it, bring it with a willing mind, and if you bring it in a teacup, it's sweeter than a pan cup. Bring it with a willing mind.

Growers and Millers Ensemble

Bring it Mr Chairman, bring it, bring it with a willing mind, and if you bring it in a teacup, it's sweeter than a pan cup. Bring it with a willing mind.

Mama Dlo

All you men like all you **cocoa tea** boy! That go make Papa Cane happy. He used to love a wake just to sing and enjoy himself.

Devine

I angry, Phyllis. I so angry these last few days, seem like a year already and I've not had vengeance for my Father's death yet. I've seen the murderer every day since, and girl, I can't tell you of the thoughts I have each time he dares to speak to me. I'm so glad Mama spoke to us all this evening. You know, if Mama Dlo wasn't there earlier today, God knows what would have happened.

Phyllis

Devine, today is just the opening credits to the rest of your life and you must live it free of guilt or bad feelings, so you must do what Mama suggests and never look back. I go always love you Devine. No matter how many years from now, my love for you will never change. You see Ruthven and all those boys in your father's veranda playing dominoes?

Devine

If any one of dem trouble you, is trouble. I don't care who it is, is a ***bull-pistle*** in he tail. One bull to ben' him. 'Pow!' And another to straighten him up. "Huum!" *[A guttural sound]*

Phyllis

Wait na! Devine, try as they might, only you hold my heart, I know you won't forget it's there, squeeze it. *[she embraces him]* Like an amoeba, split us apart for any reason and our spirits will find each other in time. I don't know why but I'm not afraid of anything as long as you are safe. I can handle Warner, but not if he hurts you. I know he only gives me special privileges cause he is thinking

notes

Suggestions on Characters, Text, Songs & Language.

***Type the following **Emoticon symbols** for audience view of **wwwpc communication between Mama Dlo & Oz, on a multimedia screen*

***(Line 12 col 3) Mama Dlo dressed in a rich apparel of royal african traditional costume, red and black beaded necklace, silver bracelets on her hands.*

(Line 11 col 4)
8 :-) Oz is a wizard

(Line 35 col 4)
I-D = Ho ho

Below:
Cocoa for the production of chocolate

he above he station for me. He ain't know me! Maybe it's time to take you' sailing and boating skills to another level. You love boating. You always talking about it. You and Norris, Geddes, even Eugene. It's in your blood to sail, just like you' Father. Another life far away from the toils of sugar cane might just be a solution to how you feel, 'til we find out who really kill Papa Cane.

Devine

Girl, I don't know about leaving you na, all these fellas like blue flies buzzing around my beautiful **hibiscus** in a garden full of plenty flowers. You making joke Phyllis, let's find another way together. I will not leave you in La Sagesse for these vultures and Warner! He best be careful **he don't lose he tail!** No matter what Mama says, better you leave with me or you work in St Lucia or Trinidad and stay with your family there, girl. No matter where the boat sails or the wind blows, your eyes, your love, strength of heart and this moonlit night will remain my compass always. There isn't a place across the Atlantic Ocean that our love can't reach.

[They embrace]
I love you Phyllis, never forget that.

*Enter **Sousin** from the veranda*

Sousin

Phyllis, girl, you've been counting the stars with Devine again; you all doing that since you were small, you haven't finished yet? I've been looking for you since Mama's **Shango**. I glad Devine brought you here early. Agree and Warner don't seem to know where day begin and night end. Your boy, Sagaboy, is in the kitchen cooking up a storm. I tell you he have a sweet hand, and the **souse**, **cocoa tea** and **rice tea** really nice. They also have chicken, rice and **stew peas**. People bring enough rum. **All you** family and good friends here and so many of Papa Cane school friends from **GBSS**. They all telling stories about Papa Cane and they school antics, and debating about rum from town and rum in de country and so on.

Bacchanal ain't even start yet. **Hear nah** Mama Dlo put down one **Oil Down**, all a we go eat 'til we **bassodie**. I really miss Papa you hear, and the people I see these past few days tells me how far his wisdom reached. So many people who loved him from my Auntie Anne to little schoolboys, that's all they talking 'bout.

*[Music: **CT Stroll** begins to play inside the house]*

Oh God boy, you en hear de tune? *[Laughter]* CT Stroll! I want Sagaboy to dance this one with me. All you coming? All you come fast!

Devine

Careful he ain't dance some kinda new poetry for you and clear the floor in he special shoes he been dying to wear with he new trousers. You know how he love to **cut style**. Phyllis, so much more I have to say. What I said before still stands but now let's stroll **we way** girl.

Phyllis

I ready for you. **Show me your motion**
*[They walk towards the house, ease the door open to join the **wake** inside]*

CT Stroll – *Dance Sequence*

*After the CT Stroll **Mama Dlo** speaks to **Devine** briefly and hastens to her house to prepare to contact **Oz**.*

*Exit **Mama Dlo***

SCENE :8

Wizzie Wizzie Web palm chat

Music: ***Wizzie Wizzie Wizzie***
Instrumental Interlude

Enter ***Oz***
Scene: ***Oz*** *fermenting his wizzie, wizzie*
brew and warming his *****wwwpc*** *by the fire*
as he brews in order to go online to find his
comrade *****Mama Dlo*** *who sits on a small*
wooden bench close to a large old copper
cauldron, roasting corn on a log wood fire.

Oz
O'er the valleys and across the seas,
o'er sugar cane fields, palm trees,
slag heaps and quarries, breathe me their
name whose powers are the same; where
fury and despair pollute the air.

Brew! Brew! Wizzie, Wizzie brew!
Stew! Stew! Wizzie, Wizzie stew!
O'er sugar cane sticks and mining pits,
sugar needs coal! Burn, burn,
energies, burn!
*[**Oz** Looks at audience, teasing with*
his lump of coal]

Crickle! Crackle! Crackle! Crackle!
Coal, coal! Sparkle, sparkle!
Miners, miners! Workers, workers!
Hither, thither! Find me Warner!
Flicker, flicker, ***Davey Lamp*** flicker!
A lump of ***sugarcake!*** A piece of coal!
Cric, crackle! Crac, crackle!
Mirror, mirror, please unfold!
Warner, Warner is needed to unite coal!

Enter ***Mama Dlo***
[On her wwwpc in Grenada]

Mama Dlo
Coal? Charcoal? This looks like a big
black crystal ball of hardened ***molasses***.
It's sweet eh! Not as sweet as my brown
sugar, but it sparkles! It crackles!
It's getting warmer!

Oz
[Juggling with his block of coal,
raises his wwwpc]

Warmer, warmer! Warner, Warner!
Coal, coal! Glow, glow!
Take me to warmer shores!
*[** Type* ***emoticon/symbols****]*
There's energy somewhere!
Sparkle, sparkle, Cric, Crac, crackle!

Mama Dlo
[singing]
Fire's burning, fire's burning,
draw nearer, draw nearer!
To the fire! To the fire and you
will be warmer!

*[**Mama Dlo** reads]*
"Welcome Mama Dlo!
Sign in here"

Oz
Warmer! Warmer!
No! Warner! Warner!
Cric, crackle! Crac, crackle!

*[**Oz** reads]*
"Sign in here, re-enter password"

Mama Dlo
*[**Type* ***emoticon/symbols****]*

Oz
Mama Dlo! Amazing! By sugar lumps!

Mama Dlo
Sparkle, sparkle, the voice of need
I sense is near!

Oz
Someone you ought to know!
O'er the hills and valleys, 'neath peaks
and 'neath the snow.

notes

***Above:** Sugar cane crusher*

Suggestions on Characters, Text, Songs & Language.

***Type the following **Emoticon symbols** for audience view of ****wwwpc** communication between **Mama Dlo** & **Oz**, on a multimedia screen*

(Line 17 col 1)
:'-) = user is so happy
:^D = "Great! I like it"

***Below:** **Cold liquor**. First stage of refining sugar where the juice is squeezed from the sugar cane.*

Mama Dlo

*[Can't see **Oz** yet. She mumbles to herself]*
Stop surfing Oz! Enter your wizzie password so I can safely chat to you on the wizzie line!

Oz

[Texting]
"wizzie wizzie wizzie dot coal dot com"
Cool! Coal!

Mama Dlo

"I have a friend online"!
Wicked, coal's here!

Oz/Mama Dlo

*[**Type **emoticon/symbols**]*
[Laughter]
"Energise. Energise".

Oz

[Still texting emotions]
Cric! Crac! That's mighty cool!

Mama Dlo *[To herself]*

Coal, now we're talking online, Time for a Wizzie chat! *[Laughter]* Wizzie, wizzie, wizzie! Cric, crac! Cric, crac!

Oz

[Looking at his wwwpc]
What's on source, sister? Toast me a corn whilst we rap pure energy.

Mama Dlo

Sugar and cane, Oz. Our work force is furious, our most respected Union leader murdered mysteriously – conditions for the planters and the factory workers under this new owner Warner, has worsened. Sackings by the hour, the **grinding stone** is the centre point of nearly all the worker's fury. I tell you, bloodshed is nearer than I can tell you. It's the people versus management everywhere.

Oz

Do you have a new leader on your plantation? Don't tell me you hold the force?

Mama Dlo

[Smiling]
Just Mama Dlo. My force.
But I could do with some of yours.
We need union cooperation!
We sure need each other to survive ***that iguana man*** Warner!

Oz

Wherever there is smoke, there's fire. The collieries are facing the same threat. The workers are sharpening their iron. It's shovels and picks. Soon will come the ***real licks***. So I need a password just for safety! There are too many hackers around. I want us to be safe and sound! And I sense movement around.

Mama Dlo

Change Site? You need to get a firewall.

Oz

Ozzie, Ozzie, Ozzie.
Oye, Oye, Oye.

Mama Dlo

Water stand up, water lie down.

Oz

Ozzie, Ozzie, Ozzie.

Mama Dlo

Oye, Oye, Oye. Water stand up.

Oz

Ay! Water lie down. Bring on the drama, Mama Dlo.

Mama Dlo

*[Monitoring movements on the Sugar Queen, watching **Devine**]*

Oz, just stay online. I'm picking up the movement 's source. On the web course. Boarding the ship, wizzie, wizzie, wizzie. He's got charcoal! Devine, he's on his way. Oz, I'll brief you later. It's the ship 'Sugar Queen' with a young man, he's quite tall, good looking. Ship sail. My goddaughter's Devine! storytelling! Captain Morgan Thomas.

*[**Mama Dlo** shaking shelled roasted corn in her hand]*

Ship, sail! Sail fast!
Captain, captain!
How many men on board?

One, two, three four!
Cric, crackle! Crac, crackle!

Mama Dlo
*[back to **Oz**]*
Yo! Brother Oz!

Oz
Who is that young man?

Mama Dlo
Just hang on! You'll see. Sugar and coal! Time will tell.

SCENE :9

The Journey by sea

Music: ***Aquamarine Bay Waltz*** *piano underscore*

*Enter **Devine, Geddes Cool, Captain Morgan Thomas** and **sailing crew***

*Scene: **Devine** on the Sugar Queen with **Aquamarine Bay Waltz** piano underscore playing, while **Devine** is telling the story of his father's death.*

Devine
The night before Papa Cane was murdered, we heard all the dogs around the house howling. Old people say the dogs does always see the spirit passing when someone in the family is dying. No one of us expected this would be Papa Cane, and during that day, the workers were wild with fury. The police had to come to protect Mr Warner. That night they burnt down one of his outhouses. You should see the sky that night. It was sky red. I had to protect Phyllis, because she was his servant. Mama Dlo was worried for her safety. You see Papa loved the sea like he loved all ah we. His dream was to become a famous seaman. He wanted to be a member of the Seafarers' Union. One thing, he never missed was we DJ Waccacks show on radio! That guy knows how to get home to the estate people, he full of love.

Geddes Cool
Ok. All you switch on the radio, let's see if we could pick up *WIBS*.

Captain Thomas Morgan
What's *WIBS?*

Devine
The radio station 'Windward Island Broadcasting Station'. That's we own station, captain, our Caribbean lifeline. It full ah soul.

Geddes Cool
It would be nice to listen to some sweet sweet music as we part from these shores. Just imagine we're leaving our paradise for the unknown.

Devine
God knows if I'll ever see it again alive.
Phyllis will never forgive me.
But, I'll never forsake her.

notes

Suggestions on Characters, Text, Songs & Language.

*** Song:* ***Sweet Brown Sugar*** *(Line 42 col 3) This song can be sung as a duet or with each of the main characters from Act 1 singing a verse or specified lines.*

DJ Waccacks
[Radio broadcast]
It's the midnight hour with your favourite DJ Waccacks, the man of the people, the show that lights up the spirits for you night cruisers. Hi, what's cooking? I've got on the turntable a real nostalgic number, **'Born to Wander'**
*[**Born to Wander** starts playing]*

A favourite of the people, the sweet singing voice of Papa Cane and the Juice Sisters. The man who sang sweet songs and told us all stories and whose dream was to sail the seas. Hope someday he'll get there. Wherever you are Papa, we love you. Stay cool! You'll never be forgotten.

*[**DJ** spins vinyl nostalgia edit - **Born to Wander** playing on the radio as the background music]*

Devine
Waccacks is something else, he is the only DJ who understands the workers, he is one of we gang and ***I goin' miss this man bad.***

Geddes Cool
Devine boy, what we gonna do when this ship dock in Wales?

Devine
Just be Cool, I'm going to look after you. The captain promised Mama Dlo that after I help with the unloading of the ship if I want to stay on for a while its OK, because the ship going other places, otherwise he would introduce me to the big boss of the South Wales Coal Miners Trade Union. I could talk me way, we bound to make it. Brace yourself man. Cool, you know something, I missing Phyllis already. God knows what going to become of both of us, because I'll have to lie low for a long time.

Geddes Cool
OK, we'll have to stay together and you got to stay under cover, don't try to make any trouble; just keep cool when we get to Wales. But man, suppose this man is a real pirate, or a relative of Captain Morgan? It could be a disguise you know.

Devine
No man, if he was the relative of the old pirate or a ***jumbie***, Mama Dlo would have told me. She is no easy woman. You ain't see how Warner 'fraid she.

Geddes Cool
Any false move he make, watch out.

Devine
Man, you could talk stupidness yes, you're the biggest coward. You better don't let him know you can't swim. You only a ***mouth champion***.

*[**Devine** pulls out a picture of his father from his jacket and looks at it thoughtfully]*

Captain Thomas Morgan
*[Looking down at **Devine's** hand with the picture]*
You loved your father madly and the picture of him is the striking resemblance of you. I've heard of his stance with the worker's union.

Geddes Cool
[begins improvising on his ***tenor steel pan****]*

Devine
Yes. Everybody says so! Papa also loved Phyllis. He wanted to bless us at one of our Shango ceremonies to give praise to the gods and goddesses. He wanted us to have at least one son and had already decided to name the child, Jazz. Papa was a great singer.

***Below**: Horseshoe Harbour, Grenada.*

notes

Voice of Oz *[Off-stage]*

The race is on, Mama Dlo. We now have to cane that cockroach Warner! He is a goner. Let's get all the forges on ***Sky Red!*** This man Warner made the lives of our whole community around Big Pit a misery. If he returns to this colliery there will be no end of problems. Kids are paid pennies to work down in the colliery. Workers wages and families are dictated by his whims and fancies. He owns everything: the bank, the post office, the pub, the grocer's - lock, stock and barrel. He is a man with no heart or dignity. No morals!

Voice of Mama Dlo

[Off-stage]

Amen! We got that iguana! Oz, we gonna fix him! It's got to be speedy before the workers at the sugar factory go on strike. The troubles are spreading like wind and fire on the sugar fields. The heat is on all sides, sugar and coal! Our Shango ceremony tonight was for Devine and Phyllis to honour Papa Cane's wishes. I'm logging off now. Pick us up around twelve midnight, Ladjablès time. Make sure your web palm on hand!

Oz

Yo!' Meantime. Sister! Respect!

Mama Dlo

Sugar cane time. More time! Bye!

*Enter **Growers and Millers Ensemble** to enact a dramatic dance sequence to the song **Sweet Brown Sugar** with **Mama Dlo***

*** Song: **Sweet Brown Sugar***

CHORUS

All day, all night trucking cane
Sweet, sweet, sweet, sweet
Sugar cane
Hoeing in the sun, in the rain
Sugar cane
Juicy, juicy, juicy, juicy sugar cane

VERSE 1

Factory make Molasses,
Rum, Brown sugar
Sugar cane
For pastry, Candy very tasty
Sugar cane
Workers sowing, factory grinding
Sugar cane
Juicy, juicy, juicy, juicy sugar cane

VERSE 2

We till the soil, grow the crop
Sugar cane
Machete, man, woman, child
cutting cane
For little money, that's not funny
trucking cane
Juicy, juicy, juicy, juicy sugar cane

CHORUS

All day, all night trucking cane
Sweet, sweet, sweet, sweet
Sugar cane
Hoeing in the sun, in the rain
Sugar cane
Juicy, juicy, juicy, juicy sugar cane

All day, all night trucking cane
Sweet, sweet, sweet, sweet
Sugar cane
Hoeing in the sun, in the rain
Sugar cane
Juicy, juicy, juicy, juicy sugar cane

*Exit **Mama Dlo, Growers** and **Millers Ensemble** leaving a pan player to play **CT Prelude** – as they exit*

*Music: **CT Prelude** Interlude.*

ACT TWO

SCENE :1

Hoof's Newsflash

Music: ***Coal Miner's Waltz***

Scene: ***Outside Big Pit Colliery***

*[**Hoof** updates the audience while the hustle and bustle of colliery life takes place in the background on stage with multi-media mining events being displayed as a backdrop on set, for all to see]*

Hoof

Croeso. Here in South Wales in Warner's colliery, the miners are restless with discontent. In the valleys miners recount the history of mining through stories passed down to them by families over many generations. Their love for the beauty of their environment, which is being destroyed, rings through the air in songs wafting from choirs far and wide.

As it happens, our man, Oz Mosis the wizard, is a keen union leader. He's a sorcerer of sorts who is active in the sorcerers' circle globally. Through their own wizzie web connection, he is able to get information to help devise a plan to strike and bring Mr Warner to trial to obtain justice for the miners, their children and their children's children.

He is into all manner of wizardry, even something called web casting. I tell you he's a wizard before his time. How he does things we may never know. He's got a soft spot for us ponies. Like us he has a sweet tooth. He loves sugar as much as his passion for coal. He'll see the miners and sugar workers get their just dues.

SCENE :2

Scene: ***Safely to shore in Wales nearing Big Pit in search of work***

Enter ***Devine, Cool*** *and* ***Captain Morgan Thomas***

Devine

This place Wales look weird and cold, man.

Geddes Cool

Just think of coal to warm up yourself and make your heart glow with fire, cause this place real dark, boy.

Captain Morgan Thomas

If you want to see dark, it is when you go down thousands of feet in the bowels of the earth, dangerous, but you will survive. Oz Mosis is a good man, plus he'll take to you once you come from another union; since the mining strikes in the USA and Africa a few years back, miners put colour aside. Ay, it will be a new world for you, but at least you're alive, rather than back home dead like your Papa Cane. God rest his soul.

Devine

*[**Devine** nods to **Captain Morgan Thomas**, then turns to whisper to **Geddes Cool** as some of the miners can be seen to be leaving the colliery]*

God boy, what the blazes are we doing in this place? I see two guys with their faces and bodies blackened up. They look just like we ***Jab Jab*** masqueraders back home.

Geddes Cool

You have good imagination and I notice you're always thinking! So what do you

Below: Headgear of the mining shaft at Big Pit Colliery, South Wales.

Suggestions on Characters, Text, Songs & Language.

Colliery related characters: *eg. Hoof and Bossy speak Standard English.*

Oz speaks both Welsh & Standard English. Oz is a chameleon in character, very witty and a staunch Trade Unionist.

***Characters in transition in age and class**: eg. Devine, Geddes, Dafydd Ironpick.*

think our chances are of getting a good job mining coal here will be? On the other hand, between them and us it could be a real competition for better looks. Some of these men look blacker than we right now. Look, look man, they even have a **"Donkey Street"** here. I only see horse-drawn carriages in the movies. Donkeys are really on the trot here!

Devine

Boy, they always say ***where horse reach, donkey must reach***.
[Laughter]

*[Led by **Captain Morgan**, they arrive at **Big Pit Colliery** where the doors of the union leader's office at the top of the colliery opens up to welcome the **Captain**, **Cool** and **Devine**]*

Oz

Welcome gentlemen, **Croeso** Captain Thomas Morgan, have a seat. Are you American GIs? You look like that fit and active lot we had here during the war; by golly, they were pretty active. In fact, I hope you can sing like ***Paul Robeson***, he's well loved in the valleys and is a champion for us miners.

*[**Devine,** holding a lump of charcoal sees **Oz** playing with a lump of coal. They look curiously at each other]*

Captain Thomas Morgan

These are men from the ***West Indian Islands***. I promised a comrade that I would introduce them to you, So I'll leave them with you. I must go to arrange the cargo for my next voyage.
See you, good luck.
'Twas a pleasure to have you on board gentlemen. Goodbye.

Geddes Cool

Thanks for everything.

Devine

Safe journey when you sail again.

Oz

Be in touch captain.
*[The **Captain** leaves closing the door behind him]*

Oz

So, gentlemen what can I do for you?

Devine

My name is Devine Cane.

Geddes Cool

And I'm Geddes Cool.

Oz

My, my, you look cold rather than cool. What are you doing here? Why did you boys leave the warm sunshine to come to this cold place?

Devine

It's not by choice, it's called necessity!

Oz

Have you ever seen a coalmine in your life?

Devine

No, what we have at home are ***coal pits*** above the ground, lots of logs we cover in a special way with earth and it burns to make charcoal, which we use to cook and bake in coal pots, and stoves. We fellas know how to survive.

*[**Devine** still tossing his piece of coal]*

Oz

That's interesting. *[Indicating to **Devine's** hand]* So what's in your hand? Can I have a look at it? *[Pause]* It's lighter than our's is. Ay! So warm! *[The charcoal glows when held clasped in the hand]* This piece has a special glow. I get the

Below: *Devine & Geddes Cool discussing money matters on arrival in Wales*

feeling it's something to do with you and it's a good feeling.

Geddes Cool

It's we chance to make a living, in order to maintain our families for the future.

Devine

I used to be a trade union leader and activist on ***La Sagesse***, our sugar cane plantation in Grenada, a powerful union with real stamina. No doubt they are still fighting for the workers. I for one wish I could do more.
[They shake hands in comradeship]

Oz

You said sugar cane trade union, do you mean the GMMWU comrades?

Devine

Yes, ***Grenada Manual and Mental Worker's Union***.

Oz

Sugar and Coal is a divine combination. I'm proud to shake your hand comrade, welcome, **croeso**. May our bond of friendship go on forever till sugar marries coal. From tomorrow you will join us to work. It's a tough job, but you'll like Wales and we will make you feel at home. The spirit of the valleys and its people have a way of growing on you quite quickly. We miners are a close bunch. We depend on each other; our lives are in each other's hands. Well, *[Looks at his watch]* union meeting. You're just in time to meet the lot of us. Just follow me young men.
[Heading towards the union meeting]
I don't doubt you must be hungry after your long journey. Bossy should be around here soon.

Devine

You see what I mean, Cool. Everything's working out. Boy, this piece of charcoal is a real lucky charm. It was a pretty woman near the spice vendor by the harbour who put it in my hand. Strange!
[Looks puzzled]

Geddes Cool

I remember her saying, "Put it in your coat pocket for good luck". It's strange how people could help others just like that without knowing.

Devine

There was something quite familiar about her though. I still can't put my finger on it. Anyway, I miss Phyllis and home man and right about now I could do with some of Mama Dlo dumplin and peas soup.

[Exit]

SCENE :3

Scene: ***Miners Union Meeting***

Dafydd Ironpick, Bossy *and other union members are in the* ***Big Pit*** *canteen singing* ***Coal Coal Coal***
[Work song dance sequence]

Song: ***Coal Coal Coal***

Enter ***Oz, Devine*** *and* ***Geddes Cool***

Geddes Cool

[Whispering to ***Devine****]*
Dem fellas could sing like we man. Singing to them is just like we sweet sounds back home. I wonder if their brass band would let me play a few tunes with them? Brass and Steel pan could be sweet you know, even though Welsh brass band different to ours.

notes

Suggestions on Characters, Text, Songs & Language.

***Colliery related characters**: eg. Hoof, Bossy speaks Standard English.*

***Characters in transition in age and class**: eg. Devine, Geddes Cool, Dafydd Ironpick.*

***Below:** Miners taking a break*

Devine

We going to dance too?

Geddes Cool

That's a way of making new friends, that's a good idea.

Oz

Comrades, good morning. First let me introduce and welcome two of our new working friends, comrades from the sunny Caribbean islands. I hear through the grapevine they are staunch unionists from the sugar cane plantations.

*[Indicating towards **Dafydd Ironpick**]*

This is Dafydd Ironpick, a man who sticks to his words like a pick sticks to coal. Next is 'Bossy', known to all as the 'Pony Queen' who is also responsible for our nourishment in the canteen. Please let her know if you'd like light refreshment during this meeting. We three are responsible for all the decisions on the coal front from housing to working conditions, safety and low pay.

Bossy

Welcome comrades! In this union men and women are judged by their honour, not by gender or colour, because down there, there's no time for superiority, animosity, or curiosity. Everyone's life depends on each other– woman, child and the pit ponies too. We look out for each other. But above all, no miner ever crosses the picket line; this is a golden rule. No ***scabs***.

Geddes Cool

We are one it seems, and we all black in the mine anyway.

Dafydd Ironpick

We miners are Jack of all trades: miners, drivers, carpenters, machinists, fitters and family men.

Devine

Cool and I are happy to join you in South Wales in the spirit of brotherhood and sisterhood. We'll do our part in the struggles of trade unions everywhere to defend our rights. We're in the same boat, man. All ah we.

*[**Devine** leads the opening of **Same Boat**]*

"We're in the same boat brother
we're in the same boat sister."

Oz

"And if you tip one end,"

Bossy

"you're gonna rock the other."

Coal Miners Ensemble

*[All stand and gather to continue to sing **Same Boat**]*

Same boat brother
Same boat sister

Bossy

Good Lord look down from
your holy place

Geddes Cool

Oh holy me what a sea of space

Dafydd Ironpick

What a place to launch the
human race

Oz

So you built me a boat with a
mixed up crew with eyes of black
and brown and blue

Devine

And that's the reason you and
I have just one world and just
one sky cause...

Coal Miners Ensemble & soloists

We're in the same boat same boat brother we're in the same boat sister. We're in the same boat brother we're in the same boat sister.

Bossy

Good Lord look down from your holy place

Geddes Cool

Oh holy me, what a sea of space

Dafydd Ironpick

What a place to launch the human race

Devine

So you built me a boat with a mixed up crew with eyes of black and brown and blue

Oz

And that's the reason you and I

Coal Miners Ensemble

Have just one world and just one sky

Devine

You and I

Oz

Just you and I

Devine

One world One world

Oz

One family

Bossy/Dafydd

One world to share

Devine/Oz

One world One world

CHORUS

You and I

Oz

Now, I would like us to agree a special donation for Mrs Beth Jones, because of the death of her husband. The children and her are going to need a little assistance. It is our duty as comrades to look after a good miner's family especially at a time of bereavement. Let's be generous towards them.
We all know that ***pneumoconiosis*** can strike anyone anytime.

Geddes Cool

[Whispering to ***Devine****]*

You see what ah mean, we better start a ***su su*** with these fellas, you know. Through that, I could look after my family back home too while we here. Man, I like these guys.

Devine

[Whispering back]

Cool it na Geddes Cool, slow down man. We first have to get in and learn how things operate here, how they like to do things, build some trust, friendship and confidence. Creep before you walk man, get what ah mean, Cool? Cool it.

Geddes Cool

[Quietly to ***Devine****]*

OK. In the meantime, I will try me luck with the cook in the canteen. She bossy man, but she nice. The fellas are talking bout ***leek soup*** and ***rook pie***. I could teach her how to roll up some ***dumplin'*** you know what I mean, spread some culture in the food. She seem nice boy. I could spice up she potato with some ***nutmeg***, pepper and ***saffron***. Who knows man, we could even save on we shopping. You know you better than me at talking; you sweet, but I cool. Don't forget the

notes

way to a man's heart is via his belly.
[Laughing]

Oz
Gentlemen, can I propose a donation of half a crown as a gesture of goodwill?
[Miners in agreement shout aye!]

Devine
*[Whispering to **Geddes Cool**]*
Don't build up false hope man.

Oz
We will miss poor Stan. I'm sure he would have said something consoling to Beth and the children before he passed away. He was one of our happiest comrades. They'd appreciate our support now that he's no more.

Dafydd Ironpick
Aye comrade, a good man's family should never suffer in life or in death.

Geddes Cool
[Whispering]
See what I mean? Family come first. Boy, we have to keep thinking family all the time.

Devine
[Whispering]
That's not how you was thinking a minute ago.

Oz
Now to deeper matters. The management have decided that unless all the workers who are on strike return immediately, all bonus will be forfeited.

Dafydd Ironpick
Forfeited my foot!

Oz
Things sounds real grim comrades. Worse, Christmas is just around the corner. Mind you, we must have our Christmas festival to celebrate our achievements, welcome new friends and make all our families and the children feel the good spirit of the season. I love Christmas dinner get-togethers… meeting the retired miners, hearing their stories, it just makes my heart warm. Let us not forget that this evil man, Warner, knows how to control our entire lives; to the point of holding all our hard earned money till we are down and out, and we end up owing our souls to the company store. Without us workers he is nothing, nothing.

Dafydd Ironpick
No way, no way, no more control, enough is enough.

Geddes Cool
Done talk, it's action in he tail.

Bossy
We'll bring down this boss, Mr Warner. We must have justice for the workers.

Devine
We have the right weapon comrades, that man must go.

*[**Devine** chanting]*
Go Mr Warner got to go

Coal Miners Ensemble & soloists
[The miners respond]
Got to go got to go

Geddes Cool
That iguana got to go

Coal Miners Ensemble & soloists
Got to go got to go

Dafydd Ironpick
That iguana got to go

Below: *Geddes Cool and Bossy in the union meeting*

CHORUS

Got to go got to go

Oz

Back to the order of business. We'll withdraw our labour. We'll bring everything to a standstill - no coal, no trains, no power generators. We'll fight fire with fire. We must meet face to face with Mr Glyn Warner.

[Mumbles under his breath]

Even if I have to use the ***wwwpc*** to its fullest extent with the help of Mama Dlo for this exploitation to come to an end.

Dafydd Ironpick

I'm ready to nail our colours on the tower of this colliery. This man is evil; he is heartless to us workers.

Geddes Cool

You can't boil molasses without fire, and factory can't make nuttin' in this place without coal. ***What sweet in goat mouth, goin' sour in its tail***. We hold the power.

Bossy

Like no honey without the bees?

Geddes Cool

Yes, sister. He money don't mean nuttin. It's we the workers that put money in he pocket. He has plenty money, but no common sense.

Oz

Now comrades. Let's organise; time to save our families from further hardships. Don't let Warner break us down. No Bonus, No Coal. No Bonus, No Coal.

Coal Miners Ensemble

No Bonus, No Coal. No Bonus, No Coal, No Bonus, No Coal.

*[**Coal Miners Ensemble** sing, **Go Mr Warner** to fade]*

Devine

Comrades, whatever you decide we fellas will stand firm together as brothers on the picket line. Oz, you're right, back home on La Sagesse sugar plantation is the same problem. I had to leave before I was killed by Warner and some of his ***mongoose men***. That Warner, he organised the murder of my father Papa Cane. He was a powerful man like you; he stood for all the sugar cane workers. We leader fall, man. This will never happen again.

Oz

Let us extend our call for assistance to the Caribbean. He owns business there. We must build our forces to include international support. It is the only way! I'll contact the sugar cane workers and others. In the meantime, slow down production! The ships, barges, trains and lorries transporting coal will all have to come out and join us to slow things down a little. Think about it and we'll meet again right here lunchtime for an update. Show our two new comrades around. Be careful with these men, they're full of tricks underground. Good luck underground Devine, you too Cool.

[Exit]

*[All disperse to work singing **Coal Coal Coal**]*

Devine

[To the audience, while walking off the stage alone]

Right now, I'm interested in what down in that deep hole in the ground. I can't imagine what down there is like. Many brave men have not survived the coal mine on account of explosions,

notes

Rock-Slides, fires, floods and illness, but I'll survive this, Phyllis. *[He thinks wistfully about **Phyllis** in Grenada]* Phyllis.

[Exit]

SCENE :4

A Night's Stroll

Music: ***Collide & Swing***
Instrumental plays in the background

Scene: ***Nightlife:*** *Pub activity, working men clubs, and strollers coming back from attending or performing in a brass band or choir for the local* ***eisteddfod*** *and choir practice.*

Devine
Ah tell you what, Cool, this place full of nightlife tonight so we goin' comb the scene to check out the actions. I heard someone say they were off to see some local poets and writers compete earlier, but it's getting too dark now to find this place. We haven't got anything else to do for the rest of the night and we were lucky to have had our accommodation all set up for us near ***Engine Row***. I've heard some horror stories about finding housing! Anyway, I wonder if these fellas play dominoes? Ah feeling lucky.

Geddes Cool
You holding any cash? Maybe we could try out a hand of cards. You good at it. I only have a few West Indian dollars man. I have to find a bank that will change them. You were lucky you had someone to help you get ready, I had nobody. I didn't have the time to get foreign currency.

Devine
Cool man, this is a pound, shilling and pence country, so we'll first check the captain for the little change he promise us before we roam. Take this two pounds in the meantime, but remember which bank you got it from, the ***su su bank***. It will only survive. You get me on the principle. And you know trust is to bust, so as soon as you get your first pay packet – pay up. No time to ***Mamaguy***.

Geddes Cool
OK man, you just cool. This place cold like hell,and it look dark and dangerous, but the hillsides and valleys look so beautiful, it remind me of the mountains home and ***Grand Étang Forest***. We have to be careful we don't run into another type of ***Ladjablès*** here. I sure this place full up a ghosts.

Devine
Ladjablès? Heh, heh! *[Laughing]*

This is the part of the world where ***Frankenstein*** lives. That's who you have to look out for here. You ever hear about ***Dracula***? And the ***Hound of the Baskervilles***?

Geddes Cool
Boy, this is Wales. All them fellas like ***Dracula*** and dem is English business. The Welsh have their own.

Enter ***Dafydd Ironpick***

Dafydd Ironpick
[Overhears the last statement and decides to startle ***Devine*** *and* ***Cool****]*
Ay, here in Wales ***Ceridwen*** may take to the skies upon her broom and descend upon you with the swiftness of a dart, like the spider does the fly. Or you may stumble upon a ball of fire. Beware the

Below: *Engine Row white washed houses. Accommodation originally built for key workers.*

devil in disguise. God made the world but the devil made coal and hid it in the innermost recesses of the earth so that he might drive man mad with searching for it.

Devine

[Answers the voice without knowing whose voice it is]

We left the biggest devil at home, that Warner. The weevil think he's wise and all ah we stupid. One day, one day **congotay**, wait and see. Time longer than rope!

Geddes Cool

Man, who you talkin' to?

Devine

You, Geddes Cool!

Geddes Cool

I didn't say a word, you sure Ladjablès eh talking to you?

Dafydd Ironpick

It's only me comrades. Just came from having a few pale ales and playing a nice game of darts at the Waterfront Club earlier. I beat Oz hands down for once. He's a chessman really.

Devine

Dominoes, is really my game of choice. Hi uh…

Dafydd Ironpick

Remember, I saw you at the meeting earlier? The rest of the lads are over there.

Geddes Cool

Ah yes, so many people we met man, but I remember you now. You said Darts? and pale ale? Man, don't sneak up on me like that with darts, talkin' bout darts, you almost frighten me! *[Laughs]*

Can we go to this pub and see if they have some of we rum and maybe we try your pale, um, what you call it?

Enter **Oz** *[Stumbling down the street towards the pub on the corner, happy after having had a few too many to drink]*

Dafydd Ironpick

Ale. Come on in. I'll show you. Pay day, Friday, would be good time to come back here, great atmosphere, leave the hardship down below.

[Beckoning to **Oz** *to join them]*
So much to fight for you know. Take housing, do you know how much I owe the company? I owe more than I earn for where I live. It's a right shame. I'm so tired of living on credit. I'm a proud man and I work hard.

Oz

[Draws nearer to hear the conversation]
You all do more than your level best.

Dafydd Ironpick

[Looks to see who's behind him]
You all right boss?

Oz

Hubble grumble. Wizzie, wizzie, just fine.

Devine

Is he alright?
[Indicating towards **Oz***]*

Dafydd Ironpick

Oh yes, he's a strong one, that Oz; if anyone can make the union work, he can. He'll make it home just fine and fast too. I really don't know how he does it. He only lives it up once in a while, usually whenever the pressure is on. He'll be off to the office before he goes home to Gweneira. I never know quite what he's up to at this hour at the colliery.

notes

Suggestions on Characters, Text, Songs & Language.

Colliery related characters:
eg. Gweneira speaks Welsh/ Standard English.

***(Line 47 col 3) [optional] Gweneira sings - **The Hands I Love** with Oz before going to bed.*

Below: *A miner extracting coal at the face with a pickaxe.*

Sometimes he's a mystery to me and the rest of the comrades. He'll sober up in no time when the cold wind hits his collar. It's a long walk but he always seems to make it back home for his bath and the chair by the fireplace that he's always talking about. Sometimes, I think he flies home on an invisible stick.

Devine

I saw a young boy in the mine today, caving you call it? So young! In such a dangerous place crawling through narrow rock space.

Dafydd Ironpick

The women work as well. Now, Hoof works with us in the mine.

Geddes Cool

Boy, I wonder how Trotter we donkey making out?

Dafydd Ironpick

I'm hoping to start a family soon. No doubt you fellas are home sick. One day we'll have to have another drink and tell me more about Grenada. Sounds like we have a lot in common. What you said about charcoal today, I would never have imagined. Cool, maybe you could join our miner's choir and maybe play your steel drum. A fascinating piece of musical engineering! I've a friend in a brass band you should meet. You've got what we call **hywl**, a wind-in-your-sails oomph

Oz

*[**Oz** talks to **Devine** and **Cool**]*

I see you are fitting in quite well already. Oh! I just had a good feeling about you two. From the moment we shook hands I could feel that glow. You'll be fine miners. Ironpick will see to that. I've travelled all over, seen many distant places and faces, but there's a rotten root here that I must dig out and it will be work well done. Trust me, I know.

*[Sings the **Coal Miner's Ballad**].*

"Been a working for coal....

Music: ***Coal Miner's Ballad***

[Exit]

SCENE :5

Gweneira Mosis at home

[SFX of the fire crackling, iron bath in front of the fireplace, ironing]

*Scene: **Gweneira** is ironing by the coal fire, quite tired. **Oz** is still not home at 12 mid-night. She has a large kettle on the fire with boiling water and food nearby – the big iron bath and towel ready and waiting.*

*[**Gweneira** looks at the clock periodically]*

Gweneira

I have no doubt that tonight his excuse would be that one of the ponies were ill and he had to be there, nurse, doctor, vet and midwife, chief cook and bottle washer. Bless him! Unless those publicans don't literally throw them out before the police come along, Oz could never get away.

[She heads over to the old-fashioned pantry with a stone shelf to set out the milk for breakfast in the morning]

I just hate having to cook and wait up all night for him to eat, so little time to talk at this hour. He'll want to talk 'til morning. I know my Ozwald, bless him. Look, now the fire needs more coal.

*Enter **Oz***

*[Drunk and happy humming **Same Boat**]*

Gweneira

Oh my word, look at the state of my husband! An Englishman's house is his castle, but a Welshwoman's house is what may I ask you, with you looking as black as a bat singing "Same Boat sister"? Oz Mosis, what have you been up to now?

Oz

Building bridges across the Atlantic. Gathering the forces in the name of coal and sugar. We're in the same boat you know.

[He heads over to the pot, uncovers it]
Highlight of the week, a ***cawl***
[He removes the ladle and licks it]
Ah! Thank you love. Where's the towel, Gweneira? Oh, I see it by the **bosh**.

Gweneira

Come on love, bach don't be tup, *[whispers* Now there's a fine Welsh word for daft.*]*
Time to scrub off the coal so you can tuck me into bed. How are the Jones getting along since Stan's funeral?

Oz

We had a collection for them today and I had a word with the miners about striking. We've a strong direction and top celebrity support this time. They'll even do concerts with the choir to help the miners' cause. If they are convinced they have a future, miners might be able to manage their own collieries in future. Who better than they themselves to do the best job?

***Oz** slumps into the chair and places his jacket on the arm; slipping off his shoes, **Gweneira** goes to the ironing board as **Oz** gets up, eats and goes to the back door to bring in the blankets washed that day.*

*[****Gweneira** sings - **The Hands I Love**]*

Song: ***The Hands I love***

***Oz** returns.[**Gweneira** & **Oz** exit to retire for the night]*

SCENE 6

Wizzie Wizzie chat

*Enter **Mama Dlo** on screen, via the **wwwpc's** messenger device to allow for an online chat. **Oz** enters the morning room with the wwwpc raised towards the light to activate his wwwpc.*

Oz

It's morning up. The future is in the hands of the beholder.

Mama Dlo

She who holds the iron knows the heat.

Oz

Hic incipit incantamentum.
Wizzie, wizzie, wizzie.

Mama Dlo

Sparkle, sparkle, sparkle.

Oz

Brew, brew, wizzie, wizzie, brew.
[Stirring his brew with his long piece of sugar cane, adding a new ingredient each time he adds to the spell]

Mama Dlo

Stew stew, wizzie wizzie stew, blow wind blow, let the hills greet the sugar cane fields. Bubble molasses, bubble, crackle charcoal, crackle.

[adds her spell ingredients to her own cauldron from the mill each time she speaks]

notes

Suggestions on Characters, Text, Songs & Language.

Types the following* ***emoticon/symbols*, so that the audience can eavesdrop on the wwwpc 'text' conversation between* Mama Dlo & Oz.

*******(Line 39 col 1)*
;-) - Winking, I'm just kidding

*******(Line 44 col 1)*
:-* - Oops!

*******(Line 23 col 2)*
:-o - Wow!

Below: *Copper pot from the mill with molasses.*

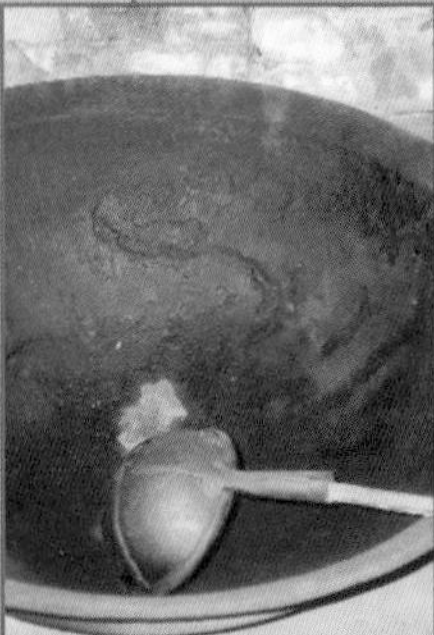

Oz
Let the fire thirst for bubbles.
All who fear will end their troubles.
*[**Oz** to his barrel to stir with the stalk of sugar cane]*

Oz
Crickle crickle, crackle crackle
Glow, glow coal glow, Sugar sparkle

Mama Dlo
Sugar sparkle, sparkle Sugar
Mirror mirror, please unfold.
[Stirring her cauldron of wizzie ingredients and sugar]

Oz
Warmer, warmer!

Mama Dlo
Water stand up!

Oz
Water lie down!

Mama Dlo
Crickle!

Oz
Crackle!

Mama Dlo
What's the crackle?

Oz
I would like to announce, guess who?
*[Holds up an effigy of **Mama Dlo** to be dropped in the barrel. Then types, *****emoticon/symbols****]*

Mama Dlo
Let's see,
*[Holds up an effigy of **Oz** and types in *****emoticon/symbol****]*
glow, glow!

Oz
Ho, ho, ho and a bottle of rum.
The miners today paid tribute to new blood. Dafydd and Devine have struck a match. They lead the strike.
Fresh flints light the way to a new future in the history of coal.

Mama Dlo
Wizzie, wizzie, wizzie brew, let fireflies crackle. When light shines, it must shine.
If out it must be all out!

Oz
Warmer, warmer. I'll reveal to our comrades deep down under all that I have heard. Eyes wide shut will soon be open. What is to be soon revealed, once sealed, will burst forth never to be forgotten.

Mama Dlo
Glow, glow, glow, the fields will see light.
*[**Types* ***emoticon/symbols****]*

Oz
Ho, ho, ho! Something's about to kick off, I see it here…
[Looks to the bottom of his wizzie barrel]

Maybe it's time to sit back and have some dessert, sprinkle some sugar on a ***crépe en flambé*** – might tickle my taste buds, set molasses to burn and make my stomach feel quite bright!

SCENE :7

Trotter's Newsflash – March on York House

*Enter **Trotter, Growers and Millers Ensemble***

*Song: **Tell the Governor***

Scene: ***Growers and Millers Ensemble*** *can be seen marching towards York House singing* ***Tell the Governor****.* ***Trotter*** *is trotting through the streets in St George's, near York House, narrating the town events as they unfold.*

Wizzie wizzie wizzie, news news news! Governing bodies have been scratching about. March on the capital to ***York House***, the House of Parliament. Demands to set the pay right.

[Quietly talks to the audience as he looks inside the window to see the Convent Girls' School activities in progress]

Boy, dey best get dem children out of there. *[Pauses, looks up]* No wonder the **GBSS** school boys always sitting on the wall! Cute!

[The children are scurried from class in single line formation]

They telling them to leave ***St Joseph*** Convent early today and go straight home. *[The children are let out of the school gate by the Nuns and can be seen running home in all directions]*

Just in time. ***Market Hill*** is ***ram packed*** with protesters. Now it's action, because the body temperature is sky high and he who plays with fire will feel the heat. The protesters demand to see the Governor-General. A workers union leader enters York House. Dissatisfied with the results, he reappears, signals with his hand and a pointed finger, march towards Leapers Hill to enact ***'Sky Red'***.

Song: ***Tell the Governor***

Exit ***Trotter, Growers and Millers Ensemble*** *singing* ***Tell the Governor***

SCENE : 8

Wizzie Wizzie strike update

*[****Mama Dlo*** *reappears]*

Mama Dlo

You see Oz? The workers are on their way to burn the fields; meantime Warner has gone bananas since our last wizzie brew. He not only ***'fraid***, he is losing his marbles 'cause he's hiding something. He's drinking so much for his ill deeds he's imagining things that never took place. Time to fix him and the cane stick he refuses to sleep without, fix him wizzie good.

Oz

Suggestion, comrade? What shall we do?

Mama Dlo

The Ladjablès should enchant and beguile Warner to leave ***La Sagesse Estate***. Later, we'll hold a ***Nation Dance*** at the ***Grand Étang*** by the beautiful lakeside. Then she will lead him to the famous ***Leaper's Hill*** in ***Sauteurs***, where legend has it that one of the last of the native ***Carib women*** leapt into the sea to avoid capture by the French invaders.

Oz

Warner has a secret of which I am aware; land ill-gotten is what drives him spare and he buries the secret in rum and ladies spare. Leaper's Hill is the place; he will reveal it there. Wizzie wizzie, get him to sign over a percentage of his estates and collieries to the workers. Give the workers the opportunity to profit from the fruits of their labour as well as negotiate better pay, housing and working conditions.

Mama Dlo

I'll have to get Phyllis away from the great house to another island for a while; she will be broken-hearted, having already lost Devine. But I have good friends on the island of St Lucia. I'm sure I can convince her to go. We have contacts there. They'll look after her.

Oz

Sparkle! Sparkle! It will soon be over. I'll help you plan the future for Devine and Phyllis. Ho, Ho, Ho! You never know. Let the fires glow sister, keep it cool. Sparkle! Sparkle!

Mama Dlo

Glow! Glow! Burn fire burn.

[Singing as she exits]

Fire is burning, fire is burning, fire fire, fire, fire… He who plays with fire will feel the heat. That ***Manicou!***

Music: **Wizzie wizzie wizzie**

Instrumental Interlude

[Exit]

Below: *Oz (left) and Mama Dlo having a wizzie chat*

ACT THREE

**SCENE :1

Warner's Escape

Suggestions on Characters, Text, Songs & Language.

*The Contents of **Warner's trunk: Gold coins, other pieces of gold and silver, tobacco pouch, old deeds, an old musket, silver watch & chain, Welsh love spoon, two blankets, bowler hat, and several thousand dollars.*

***Workers 1 2 & 3 (Line 45 col 2 and Lines 1 and 13 col 3) are intended to be ensemble members representing both Sugar and Coal*

Below:
Mr Warner In the process of disguising himself with boot polish in preparation for his escape

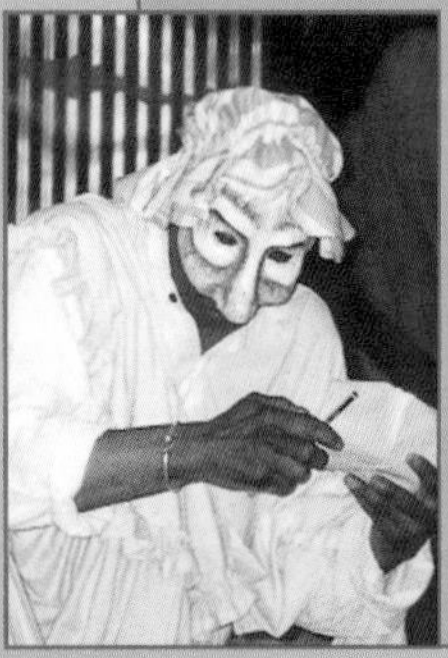

Growers and Millers Ensemble, *now an angry mob, approach La Sagesse estate, brandishing flambeau and blowing conch shells.*

Trotter
It could all be a drunken dream, but to Warner, this time it seems as real as it could ever be. His sins have come home to roost. It's time to cook the goose. In the moments to follow Phyllis will finally exact her revenge for the murder of Papa Cane, for causing her lover, Devine, to flee for his life, and for Warner's disrespectful ways with the ladies in town. Phyllis has arranged to be with Warner at La Sagesse after his visit to town, thinking that after the scene at York House, he's sure to drink himself to sleep

My master, Warner, is due for stewing. The workers go ambush the place and set La Sagesse a fire. To Leaper's Hill for confession he will spellbound go and there the sins of his past will revisit him, and his day of reckoning will come.

Fever is high. The workers are chanting ***"We want Warner, we want Warner."*** Donkeys are braying all over the countryside as they are taken from the burning fields by the workers, amid cries of Sky Red! Sky Red!

*[**Trotter** gets audience to chant continuously]*

"We want Warner, We want Warner, Warner, Warner, Warner. Better don't bolt your door cause we want Warner, Warner, Warner got to go!"

*[**Trotter** brings the chanting to a stop by contemptuously stamping his feet]*

*Enter **Phyllis***
*[Knocking on the door she sees **Warner** who is in a deep sleep on his table, snoring with a bottle of rum by his side]*

Phyllis
Wake up Mr Warner, wake up sir, the fields are on fire, fire everywhere for miles.

*[Voices in the distance shouting, **conch shells** blowing]*

Sky red, sky red! Wake up man, wake up. Come to your senses. Wake up!

Warner *[Startled]*
Agree, Agree, shoot them, shoot them. It has to be Devine's supporters and his striking mob. Like father like son. Phyllis, get me the gun.

Phyllis
Gun! Gun! Sir, Agree have the gun. I look for it already, it's not anywhere. We in trouble! Quick quick, we got to get out, they will kill us. No bullet could stop them, not ten like Agree and the gun. Put on one of my dresses, no time to scratch and smell, ***stupidie***, let's go, alé alé, let's go, let's go. Run for your life man, run.

*Enter **Growers and Millers Ensemble***

Growers and Millers Ensemble
[Shouting outside La Sagesse estate's main gate]

****Worker 1**
Warner, you mongoose, come out here, we goin' get you, we know what you do....

Worker 2

You thief the workers. Murderer, murderer!

Growers and Millers Ensemble

[Singing]

Go Mr Warner got to go,
Got to go, got to go.
Go Mr Warner got to go
Got to go got to go

Worker 3 *[Shouting]*

We goin' cook your goose!

Warner *[Whispering]*

Here's the key Phyllis. Open the trunk, take the money out and give it to me. My sugar cane, where's my cane? I must find it.

Phyllis

Mr Warner, no time for that old cane stick. Just rub this black polish on your face and put this head tie on your head and follow me. I know a short cut to….

Warner

I'll fight them, I'm no coward. No way, no way, this is my property. Boot polish! What do you think I am? A *Masquerader*?

*[**Warner** looks out of the window]*

Phyllis

You no more Mr Warner. Now, you nearly dead like Miss Anna's child, Octavia. You forget? She wasn't supposed to be working in the mill, but since you sack Mr John, and you ain't pay, the girl had to send Octavia to go out and work for she self! Octavia loose she arm a few hours ago. She caught she arm loading the cane into the crusher in the factory. Father Fields attended her and gave her last rites. If you don't hurry up he'll be attending your funeral next. Mr man, come on, follow me, they breaking up the gate. Plenty of them, oh God! Man run *nah*, run! We'll make tracks down the hill to Mama Dlo. She is me godmother, she will see after you regardless of what she feel about you. Now close your eyes, now open them, close it, again. Close out the devil! *Leh* we get going.

Warner

Never! Superstitious nonsense. What rubbish? Voodoo rubbish, rubbish.

Phyllis

You'll see rubbish! You're in trouble Mr Warner; out of the frying pan and into the fire! If we meet anyone, just say nothing, and follow, follow me.

[Mischievously]

I am your guardian angel, yes, your angel of the night to guide you swiftly in your flight from the workers' fury. I'll release you from your mind's strife.

*[Thundering chants of **"We want Warner"** in the background]*

*Exit **Growers and Millers Ensemble***

*Enter **Tuki***

*[Led by **Tuki**, **Warner** follows **Phyllis** who has just transformed into a Ladjablès as they dance towards **Leaper's Hill**]*

*Music: **Tuki Instrumental** to fade*

SCENE :2

Warner's Secret Unveiled

Trotter

Sky Red with workers fury. I done travel from St George's, over the hill to *Grand*

notes

Suggestions on Characters, Text, Songs & Language.

*****Props and settings** [Scene 2] Leaper's Hill is a glow with light from the **Growers** & **Millers** carrying flambeau, whilst the live web cast displays the light coming from the corpse-candles, Jack o' lanterns and Will-o'-the wisps in the windows of the neighbouring houses as the miners gather to voice their discontent.*

*Both the **Miners**, **Growers** and **Coal Miners Ensembles** brandish work tools and placards to bring about justice for the workers on both sides of the Atlantic.*

Below:** **Agree** (left) fighting with **Mr Warner

Étang, to Leaper's Hill. A whole two and a half-hours and I wasn't going as slow as a donkey! I was trotting in horsepower.

[He laughs and brays]

I just here awaiting the appearance of my old friends Hoof, Oz and Mama Dlo, to get he, Warner, to agree better working conditions for all a we and to summon the earliest rulers of the magical universe, who created the wizzie wizzie world fearing the growth of greed and corruption when extinction seemed eminent. Woe betide that man. Better must come. Ancient Order of King Meterolisis, ruler of our supernatural wizzie kingdom awake. Clarior-E-Tenebris. Brighter out of Darkness.

*[**Trotter** now joined by **Hoof**, gives the signal for the striking of the ancient drum. The **Doom Doom** is sounded, calling together the highest orders to attend the **Wizzie Doom** in ceremonial attire]*

Music: ***Tuki Instrumental** mix*

*Enter **Sousin, Sagaboy** and the **Growers and Millers Ensemble** who congregate, while **Tuki's special army**, responsible for preparing the court for all trials, are just finishing their duties. Three ancient scholars, **Asteroditis, Kinetisis** & **Saccharoditus** enter with **Mama Dlo**. All are surrounded by flambeau burning. The **Coal Miners Ensemble** gather to watch **Warner's** trial via webcast with **Dafydd Ironpick**, (dressed in a knitted sweater marked "Valley Boy") **Bossy, Devine** and **Geddes Cool**, on one side.*

Mama Dlo

King Sugar and King Coal, elders of the animal kingdom of the Wizzie Wizzie World of the Invisible, what are the herbal remedies for the wizzie brew?

*[**Hoof** and **Trotter** appear with an array of herbs and flowers from Wales and Grenada. **Mama Dlo** begins the incantation]*

Stew stew, wizzie wizzie stew.
Brew brew, wizzie wizzie brew.

*Enter **Tuki, Phyllis** and **Mr Warner** [in a procession followed by **Father Fields**]*

Mama Dlo

The doers of evil must always pay for their deeds.

Tuki's special army

Amen.

[Make a formation in order to guard the accused throughout the process]

Warner

I'm not evil. Who you think you are? Why have I been brought here? Why the Welsh **corpse-candles** in those windows over there?

[He points toward the houses in the webcast]

You bunch of **Grabble Phantoms** and **Babbledogs!** Talk to them Father Fields.

*[**Phyllis** turns towards **Father Fields**]*

Phyllis, don't follow them. Phyllis, come back, don't leave me alone. Phyllis, Phyllis! Birds of a feather, they flock together. Traitors! Traitors!

Mama Dlo

For your evil deeds you must surrender half of your fortune to the many children you have fathered and all those whom you've wronged and mistreated on ***La Sagesse*** sugar plantation and in your colliery abroad. Yes, Mr Warner, we have all had enough, including Oz, the miners and their families, the sugar cane workers, one and all.

Sagaboy
[Shouting angrily]
Vengeance, man, vengeance! You'll spill no more blood on this plantation, you exploiter of the poor!

Coal Miners Ensemble
Slave driver! *[All sing]*
"Go Mr Warner got to go, got to go, got to go".

Warner
Who the Dickens cares? This is my estate. I'll show them who's boss.

Sousin *[Under her breath]*
Charmed!

Warner
Don't dare charm me, who do you think you are? *[Heavy footsteps]* What was that? That sounds familiar What was that Phyllis? Answer me! Who's there? *[Nervous]*

*[**Phyllis** gives a knowing look to **Mama Dlo** and swiftly turns around]*

Agree
Ha! Ha! You...

Warner
Agree! Thank God you have arrived. Protect me.

Agree
Don't look to me for mercy.

Warner
Protect me, not them. *[Pause]*

Agree
Protect you! To think after all the years of serving your family that you could be so worthless. Your brother willed the estate to Papa Cane; that's why you killed him. I have the proof right here.

[He violently throws the cane stick to the ground. It splits, revealing a rolled-up parchment containing the will]
*[**Mama Dlo** picks up the document and passes it to the three scholars, **Asteroditis, Kinetisis** & **Saccharoditus**, for their examination]*

Warner
[In a mad panic]
Give me that document. It's my property. Give it to me this instant, you witch!

Scholar #1
Hmmm. This document has been altered.

Scholar #2
The original writing has been erased and a new text written over it. It's a forgery.

Warner:
That's a wicked lie. I'll see you in court for slander. Talk is cheap, but can you prove it?

Scholar #3:
[Holding the parchment up to the light]
Yes we can. This document is a palimpsest. It's perfectly clear that someone has scratched out the name of the original beneficiary, "Papa Cane", and written a new name, "Glyn Warner", in its place. *[Waves the document aloft, between thumb and forefinger. Hands it to **Mama Dlo**]*

Warner
It's a trick! They are working magic on the paper. *[Turns to appeal to the assembled workers]* Don't you see?
*[His exhortations are met with cries of "thief!", "impostor!", "robber baron!" and chants of **"Go Mr Warner, got to go, got to go, got to go!"**]*
I didn't do it. I didn't.....It must have been the lawyers. Yes, that's it. You know you can't trust these fellows. How was I to know, Father Fields? Have mercy on me, I beg you please. *[Falls to the ground in abject*

notes

Suggestions on Characters, Text, Songs & Language.

***(Line 6 col 1) Fight resembles a traditional stick fight.*

Both Ensembles carry a variety of placards relating their demands and expressing their discontent.

***(Line 30 col 3) The Wizzie Wizzie World of the Invisible **(WWWI)** is a mythical world located in the depths of a deep blue lake which is surrounded by a carpet of lush evergreen trees, fauna & flora. This world is ruled by an Ancient Order of scholars & mythical characters. The Goddess of the lake is **Mama Dlo**.*

*The WWWI is where people like **Warner** are banished to heal for an unspecified period, at the mercy of the wizards and sorcerers.*

***Below**: Workers on strike in Grenada*

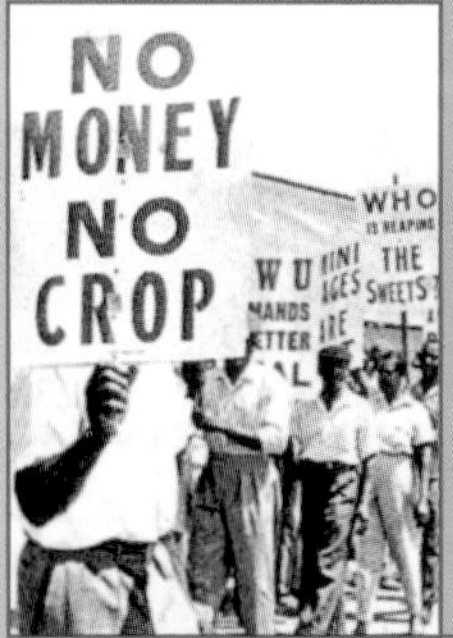

misery, his hands clasped in supplication]
Give me that gun, Agree, or I'll knock you down. Come on, you traitor.

*Music: **The Fight** Instrumental*
***[Choreographed fight between **Mr Warner** and **Agree**]*

Phyllis
It takes a sprat to catch a whale, big man!

Warner
This is treason. Not one of you will touch me. How many more of you? Agree, you're fired, fired I say.

*[The apparition of **Oz** appears]*

Oz
[Voice in the distance]
O'er the hills and valleys, what man sows, so shall he reap. Even from afar, I see you, Glyn. Aren't you ashamed of yourself?

Warner
Oz? *[In disbelief]*
Oz? You stitched this up! That could be the only reason you are present. It has been many years since I've seen your face. In fact, now I think about it, you've always had some mysticism about you.
I know you, you're managing my colliery in South Wales, but now you're here. Vengeance for dead souls and miners with the **Black lung** eh Oz? What are you? Who are you? Why aren't you looking after my property anyway? Come on, show your face, traitors, traitors the lot of you. You're all fired. Others like you come a shilling a piece. You'll not be missed. Phyllis!

*[**Phyllis** runs towards **Mama Dlo**]*
Come back! I've been good to you. You know I have. Don't you abandon me too! You are special to me, my sweet. Phyllis! Phyllis! Phyllis, not you too!

Phyllis *[Sobbing]*
A friend in need, is a friend indeed yes indeed. You destroyed everything, you've driven the only love in my life away from me. Tit for tat, butter for fat.

Warner
Oh Phyllis. Oh, No! Please forgive me.

Mama Dlo
Stew stew.

Oz
Brew, brew.

Mama Dlo & Oz
Hic incipit Incantementum

*[**Mama Dlo** and **Oz** turn to **Warner**]*
One minute to go and he'll be ready for the wizzie brew.
*[**Oz** is chomping his mouth while his lizard-like tongue lashes the air to breathe fire]*

Warner
[Sweating, breathless and forlorn]
You think I don't know that I was too greedy? I do, I know. I just have no idea how to fix it. I've been on this path for far too long. What can I do to avoid ruin? Without workers I'm spent. Without Phyllis, I'll be lost. I need…

Oz
You need to begin with the bonus for the workers and abolishing child labour, so the children can go to school. Give the workers their rights and afford them their human dignity. Ancient Order No.2: **Non Palma Sin Labore**.

Warner
Why didn't you just say that instead of putting me through all this misery! Why am I, Warner, talking to you this way? You won't break me, not one of you.

Growers and Millers Ensemble
[Chant] **"No money no crop"**

Father Fields
Look to the Lord for mercy.

Oz
Brew brew, wizzie wizzie brew.

Oz & Mama Dlo
Trouble trouble toil and trouble.
Fire burn and cauldron bubble.

Mama Dlo
Stew stew, wizzie wizzie stew.

Oz
You must surrender half your estate.
It's time the workers have a stake.

All Ensemble workers
Not a stake to the heart.

Oz
Sign this deed and in the eyes of all the spirits you will be absolved. Repeat after me: "O'er the hill and into the sea to the sharks, o'er waters aquamarine 'till I reach beyond this world, and into the *****Wizzie Wizzie World of the Invisible".***

Father Fields
[Interrupting ***Oz****]*
Surely, he should be shown some mercy! Forgive them Lord, for they know not what they do. Lord forgive us all our sins.

Warner
No! No! No! I I'll agree, I'll agree, *[****Warner****, by this time mesmerised, shrouded by the images of his evil. Then he breaks down and prepares to sign]* I will sign. Give me the deed. I'll sign. I'll sign.

Oz
Read it!

*[****Warner*** *reads aloud the promises written by the workers for him]*
I, Glyn James Thomas Warner, hereby bequeath forty percent of the shares and holdings of my entire estates: La Sagesse in the Island of Grenada and my coalmine, Big Pit in South Wales, to my workers presently working *[Under his breath]* save for that Devine. To Phyllis my former faithful servant I leave the four acres surrounding La Sagesse great house to be put in trust for her children or anyone else she chooses. All this I give in pardon for the exploitation of my faithful workers both here and abroad. So help me God. Where do I sign?

*[****Father Fields*** *sighs a sigh of relief]*

Oz
Sign here. *[Pause]* Brew brew wizzie wizzie brew.

Mama Dlo
Stew stew wizzie wizzie stew. To the wind you'll go, new seeds to sow. The fields will celebrate your retreat to the Wizzie Wizzie World of the Invisible to cleanse your liver and your soul. *[She adds an effigy of* ***Mr Warner*** *to her brew]* Thief! Murderer!

Oz
Big Pit colliery will celebrate your retreat to the Wizzie Wizzie World of the Invisible.

Mama Dlo & Oz
Over the hill and far away into space, out to the Wizzie Wizzie World of the Invisible and there you'll stay 'til time releases your pains.

Warner
Song: ***Warner's Secret (Cyfrinach Warner)*** *[Welsh Translation]*

notes

Suggestions on Characters, Text, Songs & Language.

** Trotter & Hoof *(Line 17 col 2) sing the Song* ***Tuki*** *and the* ***Spirit of Tuki*** *leads her special army and the workers in a dance to the top of Leaper's Hill. Once transported to* ****WWWI**, *(Line 25 col 2)* *Warner is accompanied by the scholars who familiarise him with its ancient laws and rules. Then, finally, he vanishes from view.*

Through the CT web palm connection the story goes on exuberantly in the *****Wizzie Wizzie World of the Invisible*** *(Line 25 col 2) with mysterious and curious figures like Oz, Mama Dlo, Ladjablès, Tuki, Trotter & Hoof using a rich vocabulary to carry out the order.*

Below:
Tuki's dance

This song is a lament. The English version of this song can be found in the song section]

Pam na cha'i gariad
Wn i'n iawn:
Devine, rwyf i'n difaru
Ga'i wneud iawn?
Lladd dy dad am dir ges gan fy mrawd
Newid y gweithredoedd i'm henw - madde'i mi.

Nawr y mae'r gyfrinach yng ngolau clir y dydd
A'r meistri siwgwr cas yn gwybod popeth sydd.

Rwy'n boddi mewn r_m ac yn boddi mewn braw
Fe wnawn i unrhyw beth i newid 'rhyn a ddaw

Ac fe wyddai Oz
Ac fe wyddai Oz
Mae ar ben.

*[**Warner** looks towards **Father Fields**]*
Father Fields, I ask forgiveness from all I have offended, including you, Father.
[He looks skyward]

Father Fields
In our prayers for young Octavia, I will ask the Lord to look after you too.

Mama Dlo
In life, what a man soweth, so shall he reap.

Workers Ensembles
Amen,

Mama Dlo
Tit for tat.

Oz
Butter for fat. *[**Mama Dlo** and **Oz** finish stirring their wizzie brew and gives it to **Mr Warner** to drink. He swallows the brew and is immediately transported to the WWWI]*

Trotter
It's fitting that Le Mon de Sauteurs is the place where Warner has met his Waterloo. This is a place of heroism and sacrifice from which Tuki, one of the Carib women jumped, whispering to her baby as she fled from the French invaders: *"They make war! Oh little one! Unwilling thou to flee! Come wake up, Come fly!"* From this very spot, she leapt to her death, clutching her baby to her breast .

Song: **Tuki

SCENE :3

Warner's banishment to the **WWWI

*[**Mama Dlo** and **Oz** can be seen to descend the cliff chanting and texting news via the Wizzie web palm, to countries far and wide]*

Mama Dlo
Wizzie wizzie wizzie, News News Extra Extra, Wizzie all about it.
Grenada Herald: 'Warner banished to the Wizzie Wizzie World of the Invisible'

Oz
Wizzie wizzie wizzie, News News Extra Extra Wizzie all about it. ***Welsh Argos: 'Warner banished to the WWWI'***

Mama Dlo and Oz
Wizzie wizzie wizzie Wizzie wizzie wizzie Wizzie all about it!

Music: ***Warners Secret*** *Instrumental*
[Exit]

ACT FOUR

**SCENE :1

Hoof's 21st Century Newsflash

Music: ***Collide & Swing***
Instrumental

Hoof
[Still wearing blinkers]
Well, It's the 21st century. We look back to the enormous changes. Most of the valley's big collieries have been made defunct. Big Pit is now a coal-mining museum and students and visitors from all over the world come in search of the past. The valleys are straddled by a network of modern roads and new industries are fast transforming the landscape of the past, that of iron ore and coal. Electric power has brought light and new life to the valleys and as you journey, the hills silently look on,

"They will remain the eyes
Ears and manuscripts
Legacies of hope
Monuments of change!"

In the valleys, you can see **slag heaps** everywhere, the dust of the emptied wombs of the mines and pictures of naked hills survive. The rivers trickle, streams and waterfalls appear and disappear. Age has taken its toll as you explore the faces of the elders.

It's a new era; a new technological society looking beyond fossil fuels, seeking opportunities. Just one active mine is left – Tower Colliery – a tower of strength, a monument, a quilt with an embroidery of our lives. New technology, new energies and new stakeholders grasping their destiny. What does the future hold for my son Grazer? Well, for those of us on four legs information is the key. We hear everything. Even forbidden thoughts are audible to our ears so we continue to travel with our ears, ever keen to the conversations that stumble across our paths. The future hoards a wealth of hidden intrigues, ingredients that will keep alive our yesterdays and fertilise our tomorrows!

Where are those who led the struggles on both fronts to defeat estate owners like Warner? What are they and their children doing?

**SCENE :2

At Big Pit Mining Museum

Music: ***Coal Miner's Waltz*** *reprise*

Jazz *is working at the museum. He's by the shelves, taking an inventory. The Museum Shop has just received new stock and a face-lift recently in addition to new artefacts and displays.*

Enter ***Luci*** *[with a few folders in her bag]* ***Dafydd Ironpick*** *and* ***Geddes Cool****.*

*[****Jazz*** *looks admiringly at* ***Luci*** *as she walks around the bookshelves]*

Dafydd Ironpick
[Laboured breathing]
Hello love. *[As he passes* ***Luci****]*

Luci
*[****Luci*** *nods to* ***Dafydd Ironpick*** *then turns towards* ***Jazz****]*
Excuse me sir, I'm looking for some information for my studies. Would you mind pointing me to the correct shelf, please?

Suggestions on Characters, Text, Songs & Language.

*****Props and settings*** *[Scene 1] Ponies and donkeys congregate outside CT Internet café with their buggies awaiting fares for the day.*

*****Props and settings*** *[Scene 2] Inside Big Pit Museum. Books surround* ***Jazz****, stacked on trolleys awaiting shelving with a few visitors and researchers walking through.*

Characters in transition in age and class:
eg. ***Luci Duport***
Predominantly speaks mixed Creole & Standard English

Predominantly speaks Standard English
eg. ***Harry, Jazz, Ironpick, Meurig, and Grazer***

Below: *Slag heap, part of the landscape created by coal mining*

Jazz

Hello, you said study. What's the subject and what type of information are you looking for? Give me some idea.

Luci

[Pulling out papers from her bag]

Sorry, this is not the one. Oh no, don't tell me I forgot my book list. OK sir, to begin with, I am studying "Bio-technology".

Jazz

Please call me Jazz. What a subject! That's not too difficult for me to find. *[To **Luci**]* I won't be a minute. I'll be back.

*[**Luci** goes off to look around]*

Geddes Cool

Can I have some assistance please? I'll like to buy this souvenir mug, and could you wrap it for me?

Jazz

[At the till]

It's three pounds ninety nine.

Geddes Cool

Is that all?

Jazz

*[**Jazz** nods]*

And how would you like it packaged?

Geddes Cool

[Smiling]

Wrap it with some care, love and affection, man, and put this card in it. And a nice little pom-pom. It's for a very special friend of a friend from the Caribbean.

*Enter **Meurig Cool** and **Harry Ironpick***

[Looking around]

Meurig Cool

*[Looking at **Geddes Cool**]*

Hallo Dad.

Geddes Cool

Hallo me lad.

*[Jokingly to **Jazz** at the counter]*

Thank you Mr Jazz. Man, you made a nice job of it, you are a lad with style, you full of haste, but you've got taste.

Harry Ironpick

*[To **Jazz**]*

See you tomorrow at Common threads. You know where I mean? The old coffee house.

Jazz

OK, we'll catch up there.

*Exit **Geddes Cool***

Luci *[To **Jazz**]*

I overheard that man.

Jazz

Who? You mean Mr Cool?

Luci

I don't know who he is. I am a stranger here, but he mentioned something about the Caribbean. I'm from the island of St Lucia.

Jazz

Oh yes, well, he is a regular. He's got a great sense of humour too, makes all the miners who come through here laugh. Geddes Cool and Harry Ironpick are very good friends of me Dad. We all feel sorry for Mr Ironpick though, he's poorly with ***pneumoconiosis***, what we call ***Black lung***. He has a terrible time breathing.

notes

Suggestions on Characters, Text, Songs & Language.

*****Props and settings** [Scene 3] Ponies and donkeys congregate outside Common Threads Internet café with their buggy carts awaiting fares for the day. Newspaper stand and Big Pit Museum near by.*

***Characters in transition in age and class:** eg. Bray coming towards CT café with his buggy*

Predominantly speaks Standard English [Does not wear blinkers. Adorned in contemporary bridle along with and other contemporary accessories for the cart]

***Below:** Entrance to Big Pit Mining Museum.*

Luci

Ah! Sorry to hear that. Well, my thesis is called "Common Threads". It's about the industrial similarities of sugar and coal production.

Jazz

You're not serious! Sugar and Coal? Common Threads? I can't believe it. That's the name of a trendy Internet café my mates invited me to tomorrow. I've not been in there before. How strange. *[He pauses]* Hang on a bit. Let me attend to this other man and I'll arrange something for you in no time.

*[Attending to **Meurig Cool**]*
Right, Big Pit mug and Coal mug?

Meurig Cool

No. Just this mug, Jazz.
[Smiling uncontrollably]
I like the words on it. "Love glows with coal!" What you think?

Jazz

Sounds good. Someone came in for a large order of them earlier. They are very popular. Would you like me to wrap it for you?

Meurig Cool

No! No! The truth is, it's for the girl you were speaking to. I don't want her to think I'm nosy, so please give it to her for me, will you? Just wish her good luck. See you tomorrow at the café. There are growing opportunities for coal to "fill the gap" between 2005 and 2050. That reminds me, I 've got the Miners' Union meeting next week. So much to tell you, don't miss our meeting, Ok?

*Exit **Meurig Cool, Dafydd** and **Harry Ironpick***

Jazz

*[Holding the cup on his way back to **Luci**]*
It's very busy today, often it's quite quiet around this time. The gentleman who just stepped out paid for this and asked me to give it to you.

Luci

*[Sucks her teeth to make the sound of a **steups**]* To me, why? He doesn't even know my name.

*[**Jazz** looks at her inquisitively]*
I'm Luci. I'm just a stranger. I have no idea who that man is. There's always another one wherever I go. Men! Nice mug though.

Jazz

Mug! That's the company Chairman of Tower Colliery! Meurig Cool kept coal on the map in these parts and around the globe. The only mine left in South Wales in fact and owned by miners! They're surviving quite well in the global market place. So much competition from abroad though. Have some mercy on the guy, he is just being nice, welcoming you in fact, plus we are all mates at Big Pit Colliery. We're a very close knit community. Our fathers all worked in Big Pit. Two of the people you may one day have to interview are Meurig Cool and Harry Ironpick. We call him Pick. His father's nickname was Pick. Just got handed down. Anyway, Meurig is one of the four members of the buyout team for Tower Colliery, and highly regarded.

Luci

[Looking at the shelves]
Great, I stand corrected then.

Jazz

I see you are admiring the lamps. It's the traditional Davey lamps that the miners used in the old days.

Luci
It reminds me of the lanterns we use at home.

Jazz
Can I make you a present of one of them? Take this as a souvenir from Big Pit.

Luci
Oh, you're so kind. Are you sure? I like it. I'll look after it. Thank you. But now I need to get back to Cardiff and the next bus is in three minutes. Can I come back tomorrow with my book list?

Jazz
I'll do better than that. If you don't mind, I can meet you tomorrow at the Internet café, it's my day off. I just have to see my father first. Take my card, give me a call later and I'll tell you how to get there. Take care Luci.

*[**Luci** picks up the mug, smiles at the inscription and leaves the museum, singing **Love Glows with Coal**, on her way to catch her bus]*

Song: ***Love glows with coal***
[Passers by join her for the chorus section of this song]

**SCENE :3

Bray's Newsflash

Bray
Now, as it happens, I remember Papa Cane's wish. By the look of things, Oz and Mama Dlo do too. They've arranged to be at Common Threads Internet café in a wizzie jiffy for another wizzie brew. The brew they've been concocting for two generations is about to boil over in sweet molasses, burning hot like coal fire. And guess what? The love affair which Mr Warner destroyed in Grenada will blossom with time, and union solidarity has brought prosperity. *[brays]*

As for me, the newsflash on the sugar situation around the world is that sugar's future lies in its extended use in products like paper made from bagasse, animal feed, bio-plastics and ethanol.

I won't be surprised to see our ageless wizard, the funky Oz as DJ Oz possibly, spinning wax with the max for the next rave. He'll be eavesdropping no doubt, can't help his wizzie self. Wonder what we'll hear, or what he's fixed for this generation's wizzie brew in the mix?

Now who else am I forgetting to mention? Can't forget Mama Dlo, now a delegate for Grenada who has wizzed into the UK to attend an international sugar seminar. I happen to have given her a ride to Common Threads on her search to check up on old friends, so look out for the hostess with the mostess when she takes the wizzie mike as an island DJ with a few surprises. Be on the alert and don't forget to look for me, Bray, son of Trotter, King Sugar. Almost time to trot – young Grazer's on the hoof.
[brays]

Grazer's Newsflash

Grazer *[neighs]*
Common Threads Internet café, the live joint, formerly a young people's coffee house, the in scene in South Wales. It's wicked, large, loungey and fun. It's a happenin' scene for everyone. Even my father Hoof loved this place.

[Looking through the large windows]
It has sofas and tables, iron chairs and old

Suggestions on Characters, Text, Songs & Language.

*****Props and settings** [Scene 4] CT Internet café complete with IT facilities, old mining artifacts, picture wall, and performance area with Steel pan. A poster saying **'Watch out for the surprise Web cast' www. wizziewizziewizzie.com.** A video screen and fireplace*

Older mining characters: Devine Cane, Dafydd Ironpick, & Geddes Cool

Characters in transition in age and class: DJ Oz, DJ Wiz, Jazz, Meurig, Harry, & Luci

Characters speaking Standard English & Welsh: DJ Oz, DJ Wiz, Jazz, Meurig, & Harry

***Below:** Grazer's newsflash outside CT Internet café*

mining antiques all over the place. It's the main hang out for us donkeys who make the tourist buggy run. Life's much easier working this gig. I see daylight instead of being stuck in the pit. I can have a laugh, just checking out the poetry nights and live bands, and read the papers, no blinkers. Sometimes Bray and I meet over a drink, to discuss the environment and how the taste of the grass in the countryside has changed. Anyway, today, Meurig and Harry have agreed to meet here to prepare new strategies for the only existing deep mine, Tower Colliery, and to get an update from Jazz about his dictionary of mining terminology. *[Peeps through the café entrance]*

According to the poster inside, near to where Jazz is, there's some surprises in store if you go online, and a live webcast too. Well, it's all right for some. *[Opens the door to reveal the inside of the café]*

**SCENE :4

Inside the Common Threads Internet café

*Original memorabilia decorate the walls. **Harry** and **Meurig** are sitting on a lounge sofa talking while a CT waitress serves them drinks in café's Love glows with Coal mugs. **Common Threads Ensemble** cast members are dispersed around the café chatting, drinking, eating and busily using the computer stations.*

Harry Ironpick

Injuries on the site have declined, for which we are thankful, and efficiency gains have reduced the CO_2 emissions by 40 percent, you know Meurig. By the way, what did Jazz say is happening with the mining dictionary of terms and industrial service links that he's working on? I forgot to ask him about it before he left to get a drink a minute ago.

Meurig Cool

So many comrades are asking for it, Harry. The muckers are really into it and the research interviews have given such fantastic results that we need to press ahead with getting it finished and delivering it to the miners as part of their concessionary bonus this year.

*Enter **Luci** Looking for **Jazz***

Hey Harry! Pick! *[Nods towards **Luci** coming into the café]* Looks like a great opportunity for us to marry the two – sugar and coal. Kind of life studies; those two could get up to combining quite a lot of terminology. What a proposal! *[They both laugh]*

Harry Ironpick

Ingenious prospect. You tried to give Jazz a hint when you bought that "Love Glows with Coal" mug. Maybe he took the hint.

*Enter **Jazz***

Luci

Hi Jazz, I'm sorry I'm late. I'm having difficulty finding my way around Wales. It is such a big place especially in relation to St Lucia, even though it's just as hilly.

Jazz

I should have offered to pick you up. It's my mistake; let's have coffee before getting down to work.

Luci

I don't want to take up too much of your time but I'm thankful for your help.

notes

Jazz

Don't worry about it. Relax.

Harry

Man, I think we better make ourselves scarce. See you later Jazz.

Meurig Cool

See you later Luci

Jazz

What have you been doing today?

Luci

I've been all over the place sightseeing in Blaenavon.

Jazz

You know the landscape surrounding Big Pit Colliery, Blaenavon, is one of the best places in the world to see what a landscape created by coal mining and iron making actually looks like.

Luci

Then I went to the other big museum.

Jazz

You mean the ***Valley Inheritance Museum***? I used to work there before coming here.

Luci

Really? Do you know, by some strange coincidence I came across an elderly lady there and she told me to visit Big Pit. That's how I got to meet you. She said she knew someone at Big Bit and to tell you the truth, I think I'm losing it! Cause I'm sure I just saw someone like her outside on a sightseeing buggy as I came in.

Jazz

You did? Umhum. Speaking of which, I'd love to take you for a ride on a donkey or pony one of these days.

[Looking around the café]

Describe this woman to me. I wonder if she's still around?

Luci

She is short, grey headed and about sixty something, but still quite pretty and agile. Reminds me of my Mum a bit.

Jazz

Amazing! That's about the age of the lady my father sometimes speaks about from Grenada. I've never met her. Can you spot her in here now?

[They both look around the café]

Well, anyway, it seems so strange to toast your welcome with coffee. Still, let's drink a toast to sugar and coal, especially since you're using one of the mugs we sell at the museum! Cheers!

[Both Laughing]

Luci

"What does that poster say over there?" *[pointing]* "Log onto www.wizziewizziewizzie.com?" There's a surprise in store, it says. Well, this may be just the place where we find out what the future has in store for us. I want to work as a sugar technologist specialising in industrial arts and applied sciences.

[Both logging on]

*[**Luci** reads an email from a sugar site answering her question on the use of **bagasse** in the cane fields. She reads it out loud]*

From: Dr Vicente Crow

To: Luci DuPort

Subject: Bagasse

"Dear Luci,

As far as I can tell, there isn't much research on this subject. However, years ago, I did hear of

Suggestions on Characters, Text, Songs & Language.

*****Props and settings** [Scene 5] DJ Oz is featured throughout this scene. He works his turntables and is surrounded by his collection of classic records and equipment, in between wizzie communications and radio broadcast with DJ Wiz*

(Line 27 col 4)* ***'Born to Wander' *also features on the radio broadcast,*

This suggests DJ Oz plays a short excerpt of the song. [Act 1 Scene 9]* ***The Journey by Sea* *during Devine's voyage from Grenada on the Sugar Queen.*

Below: *Jazz & Luci on a laptop at Common Threads Internet café with a steel pan in the background.*

ploughing — Vertical *mulching* combined with bagasse... I have a colleague in Cuba who may be able to help you...You see, trash normally rots in a season...."

I might just get a degree with Honours with this titbit of info.

Jazz

Amazing! Where's the best site to go to find out about the harvesting of cane and its manufacturing?

Luci

Here, I'll show you. *[She leans over]* It's interesting how they are developing the use of bagasse in the generating of electricity.

Jazz

Interesting that you mentioned that. I'm told that every room in the Savoy Hotel in London used to have a coal fire before electrification. The old coal storage is now a cosy pub. I'd love to take you there sometime for high tea.

Luci

I'd love to go

Jazz

I wonder when the live webcast will start? More surprises, I bet.

Luci

Let's log on to www.wizziewizziewizzie.com and see. *[Snuggles closer to **Jazz.** They both continue to check their emails]*

Jazz

What language is that email in?

Luci

My native French creole. I'll teach you sometime if you help me with my Welsh.

Jazz

With pleasure.

*Enter **Mama Dlo** working by the bar and **DJ Oz** communicating with her. Once he reaches his turntable and mixing desk, they recharge their web palms for the night's action.*

*[**Oz** spins a vinyl track from his collection and they begin the spell. Meanwhile, **Jazz** and **Luci** are still online]*

Music: ***CT Prelude*** *reprise*
*[**CT Prelude** is heard briefly and then fades]*

Oz

*[Behind the bar with **Mama Dlo**]*
Brew, brew, wizzie, wizzie brew
[Pours a drink]

Mama Dlo

Stew, stew, wizzie, wizzie stew
[Pours a drink]

Luci

Bingo! It's a net radio launch and we're on with a link up to the Caribbean! I can't take it! That poster wasn't kidding.

Jazz

[Laughing]
Luci, Luci. Just look at this email. Read it.

Luci

[Reading the email]
"Luci my dear, there 's a crackle in your horoscope and a sparkle in your heart. Guess what?"

*[Turns to **Jazz** in mock annoyance]*
Jazz, what could all this mean? Having fun, aren't you?

Jazz

Oh no, I'm not. But just for fun, c'mon, let me see your eyes.

Luci
No, get off.

Jazz
Come on, love. I'm a fortune teller, trust me. I want to read into your future.

Luci
You want to read into my future? Jazz, this is no hocus-pocus. This is serious business. Stop kidding.

[Strange voice from the computer]
*"**Jazz**, when you see your father later, please say hello. Tell him I will always be there".*

Jazz
[In a puzzle]
This must be Harry or one of the others setting us up. They must have fixed the computer. These guys are wizards, you know. They are good at this cyberstuff.

Luci
*[Still embracing **Jazz**]*
If that happened at home, someone would think it was witchcraft.

Jazz
Don't worry, love. Nothing supernatural is happening here.

**SCENE 5

The DJs' Mix

DJ Oz
This is the wizziewizziewizzie.com coming to you live from Common Threads Internet café, the hot spot. Welcome to the station of the nation. This is the calm before the storm. Put your minds in gear for some crazy sounds going straight to the headgear. I'm DJ Oz, sending greetings to all at the Tower.

Thanks to all of you who wrote to share your mining experiences before the turn of the century. Especially one young lady whose great granddaughter is in the audience tonight. Yvonne wrote in to tell me that her great grandmother, Edith, had to wear a belt round her waist in those days while working in the mine, and a chain passing between her legs. I can't imagine women even thinking about that in Europe today! She says she used to work on her hands and knees even when she was in the family way, went home, had the baby, and returned to her shift the next day! That's woman power for you!

This one's for you too, my love. Thank goodness that kind of thing is over. We just have to work on the bonus, don't we lads? Later, we'll be joining our international link across the seas. So here's a song with deep nostalgia. While you savour your almond coffee with Demerara sugar and sip your tea, relax and enjoy 'Born to Wander', a revival hot wax.

***Song: **Born To Wander** *edit*
*[The nostalgia mix is heard briefly – the following lyrics catch **Jazz's** ear]*

As a boy I would stand
And watch the ships go sailing
Into the harbour every day
On the hills I would be
But my heart would be a-sailing
With the ships that were
sailing away

Guess I was born to wander
(I was born to wander)
I was born to go
Where the four
(Where the four winds blow)
Never know what lies oh yonder
But I always wanted to know
I'd stand and watch the waters
clearing

notes

Suggestions on Characters, Text, Songs & Language.

Older mining related characters: *eg.* ***Devine Cane, Dafydd Ironpick, Geddes Cool***

Characters in transition in age and class: *eg.* ***DJ Oz, DJ Wiz, Jazz, Meurig, Harry, Luci***

Predominantly speaks Standard English & Welsh: eg. ***DJ Oz, DJ Wiz, Jazz, Meurig, Harry,***

Predominantly speaks mixed Creole and Standard English eg. ***Luci, Devine, Phyllis, Mama Dlo***

(Line 46 col 2)
**This suggests* *DJ Oz* *plays a short excerpt of the song.*

Below: ***Meurig,*** ***Jazz*** *and* ***Luci*** *at CT Internet café*

As they raced out into the blue
I'll stand and watch always believing
That one day I'd be leaving too

Jazz

[On his feet]

What's going on? This is one of the songs my father sings all the time. He said it was the last song he listened to while he was on the ship 'Sugar Queen' on his way out of the Caribbean to Wales. I could never forget this jam.

*[**Jazz** begins to sing along with the vinyl version and soon **Common Threads café Ensemble** join in and perform a seemingly improvised dance sequence]*

CHORUS

Zab ba da ba dap
Ba daba da ba daba dap
Zab ba da ba dap
Ba daba da ba daba dap

Now that I've sailed on many
an ocean
Up and down the seven seas
Well I guess this ain't no notion
That my home lies in the breeze

CHORUS

[All applaud themselves and disperse to their respective tables]

Luci

*[Speaks as **Jazz** returns to his seat]*

So, you're a singer too! Nice voice, but seriously Jazz, is this place real? What's really going on here?

[She shivers]

This place feels quite spooky.

Jazz

[Out of breath and a bit surprised at himself]

I have no idea, this is not a place I've frequented; but I thought you said you were inquisitive and adventurous. It's probably all your doing. I must be the odd one out. Don't blame me.

Luci

[Laughs]

OK, log off. It's too spooky. Let's chance another coffee. It's my turn to treat you, and for being such a fun guy I brought you a special treat.

Jazz

Another surprise?

Luci

No, it's just something sweet, a product of our sugar cane.

Jazz

[Holding the sugar cake]

It looks like a flaky lump of coal but light brown. Are you having me on?

Luci

No, I wouldn't do that; go on, be adventurous, taste it. My mother used to make them. She taught me the recipe. It's sugar cake. She made this specially and sent it for me and I'm giving some to you.

*[**Jazz** sees **Meurig** and **Geddes Cool** approaching]*

Jazz

[Whispering]

I'm sorry Luci, look who is here, it's Meurig and Geddes. Bad timing guys.

Geddes Cool

Can I offer you two a coke or coffee. ***Café con Léche*** or tea for two? What's your choice, Mr Jazz?

*[**DJ Oz** spins a record]*

Music: ***Love Glows with Coal*** *edit

[Instrumental softly in the background]

Meurig Cool
Hi Jazz! I didn't make you all out at first. *[Laughing nervously. Reads the inscription on the mug and sits down]* 'Love Glows With Coal'. I recognise that mug!

Luci
Mési, it's quite a handy gift. I'll always remember you.

*Enter **Dafydd** and **Harry Ironpick***

Are these two inseparable?

DJ Oz
Surprisssse!
*[**Mama Dlo** appears in disguise with a fabulous birthday cake for **Jazz**]*

Dafydd Ironpick
Happy birthday, man. Thought we'd forget, did you? *[All sing "Happy Birthday", adding, "Why was he born so beautiful." They cut and share the cake]*

Meurig Cool
And we got you a present too – a trip for two to the donkey sanctuary in Devon.

Jazz
[Laughing] Is it organic?

Geddes Cool
We know how you always go on about Bray's and Hoof's welfare.
[Mock braying]

Jazz
What a pair you two are. I don't know what to say. Thanks guys.

Luci
I promise I knew nothing about this. What a night. I'm as shocked as you. Happy birthday, Jazz. What an evening. It's really getting warm in here. Have you noticed?

[Blushing, begins to fan herself]

[Music fades]

DJ Oz
[Overhearing]
Wizzie, wizzie, wizzie, it sure is!

*Enter **Devine***
[To wish a happy birthday to his son]

Devine
Happy birthday, son. I'm proud of you.

Jazz
Thanks Dad. Oh, Dad, meet Luci, she's from the Caribbean.

DJ Oz
[At the turntable with mixing desk]
You're back with DJ Oz linking up live with the Windward Island Broadcasting Service – WIBS. Welcome back lovers, welcome to your favourite hot spot with DJ Oz. I'm hot on coal and sweet on brown sugar.

DJ Wiz
*[Played by **Mama Dlo** in wizzie disguise]*
You are linked to the wavy shores of the Caribbean, broadcasting on www.wizziewizziewizzie. com.

Luci
Jazz, Jazz, this is our radio station at home.

DJ Oz
Stay tuned for some tantalising news and surprises, past present and future. For some it may be too close for comfort, for others nostalgia breathes relief; it's your choice. This is the opportunity our internet café affords our listeners once a year to link-up with friends across the sea. Surprise begins from here.

Suggestions on Characters, Text, Songs & Language.

**(Line 39 col 2) This suggests DJ Oz plays a short excerpt of the song.*

***(Line 18 col 3) From here to the end of the scene all songs featured by DJ Oz are short but recognisable sound bites of each selection.*

This is Oz, your favourite DJ. Tonight is the night we have a special programme to find missing links and lost lovers.
Let's greet the world.
Who is calling? Who is going to smile tonight? And who will be the lucky one?
I feel spicy tonight.
Welcome to Oz's moments of deep revival sounds. Dig the vibes.
Let's see who's on line?

Phyllis
Hello, my name is Phyllis.

DJ Oz
Where are you calling from, Phyllis?

Phyllis
The Caribbean Island of Grenada.

DJ Oz
Grenada! Isle of spice where all blends nice! It's good to have you with us sister, stay on the line. Let me remind all our listeners that this is the station where big surprises blossom, so who knows, it could be your night.
Go right ahead Phyllis. Sail on, sister.

Phyllis
To tell you the truth, it's my first time speaking on radio.

DJ Oz
Don't worry sister, there's always a first time in life, you're in good hands.

Phyllis
Well, I want to send loving greetings to a long lost friend who went away, a long, long time ago.

DJ Oz
Could this be an old spark? Just who is he? Let's add some coal to this fire!

Phyllis *[Laughing]*
His name is Devine, he is tall, dark and handsome. He left and went to Wales and that was the last thing I knew of him.

DJ Oz
Old firestick!
*[Emoticon exchange between **DJ Wiz** and **DJ Oz** which can be viewed on screen]*

DJ Wiz
Sparkle, sparkle.

DJ Oz
Crackle, crackle. You say your name is Phyllis?

Phyllis
Yes. He will remember me as Phyllis Duport. We both used to work at La Sagesse sugar cane estate. That's where we knew each other.

DJ Oz
And his surname?

Phyllis
Cane.

DJ Oz
OK. Request going out to Devine Cane. Let it all out, sister. Let me add a dust of real nostalgia to spice up the night air. If music is the food of love, I'll play on. Lordie! Lordie! I'm feeling spicy. Here is an oldie for the goldies, one of my wife's favourite too, "The hands I love".

*Song: **The Hands I love***
*revival mix *edit*

DJ Oz
*[While the record is playing, **Devine** makes his way to meet **DJ Oz** in tense anxiety]*
Hang on to your seat belts folk, taste the brew in the stew. Hmmm!
The breeze in the whizz!

***Below:** DJ Oz's revival 45*

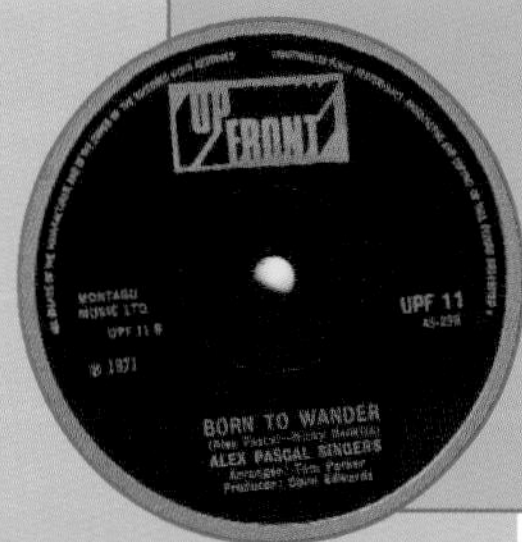

Devine

Mr DJ man, you trying to kill me! I know this song, it's one of my old favourites. Yes, man. Wow! This couldn't be my Phyllis! My Phyllis! Phyllis? I can't be hearing right! This must be a miracle. Phyllis! Is this serious? What's going on man?

DJ Oz

You never know what's in the brew. Something old, something new.

*[**DJ Oz** sings]* Fire burning, fire burning, draw nearer, draw nearer. Easy brother, easy!

***[**DJ Oz** spins another track– **Aquamarine Bay Waltz** *edit]*

Surprise, surprise! The night air is full of good surprises. Wonders never cease.

*[**DJ Oz** hands the headphone and mike to **Devine**]*

Devine

[On line] Phyllis? You said your name is Phyllis?

Phyllis

Yes, Phyllis is my name.

Devine

Phyllis! Well, my name is Devine, Devine Cane.

Phyllis

Lord have mercy! Devine Cane. I can't believe this. You still alive?

Devine

Well, I'm a little old in the bones, but I'm still here, girl. And how are you?

Phyllis

How am I? How am I? I can't believe what I'm hearing. You expect me to believe you care about me, you unfaithful man?

Devine

Please, Phyllis, please don't rebuke me. I beg you to give me a chance to explain myself.

DJ Oz

I can understand how it feels for both of you. Take time to talk it over. Time is a healer

Phyllis

Just imagine me looking for you Mr Devine after all these years, and you never ever try to find out whether I was dead or alive; not a letter, not a postcard, not even a message. Shame.

Devine

Phyllis, time is a healer. I will do anything to make it up to you. Please forgive me, I could explain.

Phyllis

To the forgotten? I had to leave Grenada, and go to live in St Lucia with cousin Ambrosine to save my life after I help to get you away. You forget who I was Devine? Your girlfriend! Devine Cane you were the only boyfriend I ever had.

Devine

Alright Phyllis, don't go on so.

Phyllis

Don't go on how? Have you forgotten Mama Dlo, Sousin, Sagaboy and all the others? Is they who saved your bacon from that cruel Mr Warner. You forget?

Devine

No, girl. I ain't forget nothin'. Tell me about yourself.

notes

DJ Oz
It's good to reason.

Phyllis
I have a daughter now. She is studying Biotechnology at a university in Wales.

Devine
You have a daughter?

Phyllis
Yes.

Devine
Studying in Wales?
And the father?

Phyllis
[Tongue in cheek]
Hmmm, typical. Good question.
Well, Mr Devine, I kept to our promise in vain for donkey's years and although this is not your business now, since you ask, I goin' to tell you straight: it's Agree.

Devine
[Yelling in amazement]
Agree! Agree! Adolphus Agree!
What a two-face, double crossing traitor. *[Steups]* I should have known that watchman was a snake. Well, I only have myself to blame. You're right, Phyllis, time waits for no man.

Phyllis
Neither do women.

DJ Oz
Revelation! Revelation! Confession is good for the soul.

Devine
I also have a child too, you know. Yes, a handsome young man. His name is Jazz. He's right here now. I just came along to wish him a happy birthday, and lo and behold this commotion began. Lord!
Oh Lord! I can't tell you how I feel. Oh Phyllis! I still love you. No matter what happened, I will always love you.

Luci
*[Holding onto **Jazz** in astonishment]*
Jazz, Jazz, oh Jazz. That's my mother.
*[**Jazz** embraces her]*

Jazz
What's going on, Luci?
[Rises and approaches his father]
Dad, what's all this about?
Tell me, dad. Tell me!

*[**Devine** embraces **Jazz** and steps aside]*

Devine
Come son, I can explain everything.
Nothing to be ashamed of, it's all fate.

*[**Devine** and **Jazz** exit as **Luci** asks **DJ Oz** if she can go on line to talk to her mother]*

Luci
Mum, Mum, its me, Luci.

Phyllis
[Sobbing] Luci, Which Luci?

Luci
It's me, mum. Your daughter.

Phyllis
Luci, what are you doing there?
How did you get to meet these people?
Lord! Lord! **Bon je seye**!

DJ Oz
Surprise! Surprise! What a night!
This is a night of surprises, the night of all nights. You never can tell what's in the stew on a party night when the wizzie wizard is out to play. Let it glow, let's keep the fire alight.

Suggestions on Characters, Text, Songs & Language.

*****Props and settings** [Scene 6]*
Waiters and waitresses go back and forth, taking orders and serving beverages along with chicken barbecued on the coal fire.

***Below**: A glowing coal fireplace*

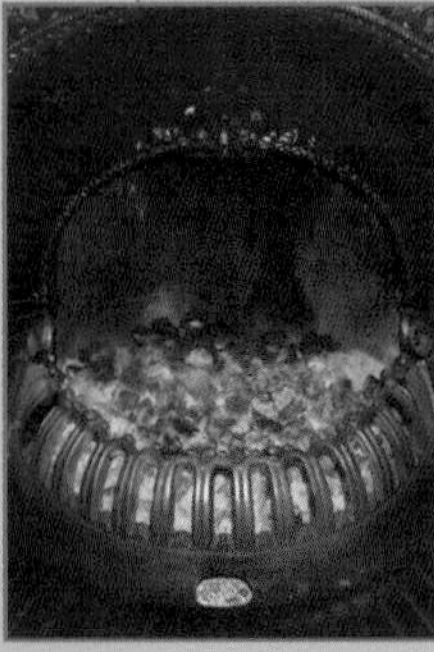

Near or far away, the energies of sugar and coal will unite. Bubble, bubble, bubble, brown sugar bubble. Fire burn and cauldron bubble. Whey horse reach, donkey must reach.

*Enter **Jazz** walking towards **Luci***

Jazz

Fate has planned this. I …

Luci

Remember that sugar cake I gave you?

Jazz

Yes! *[Smiling]*

Luci

Can't you see how talking to my mother has affected your dad? Just look at him. Look at us.

Jazz

This is a big surprise. I never knew it was such a deep affair. I'm sure you and I can work this out together.

Luci

[Laughs]

We'll have plenty of time together, I hope. Maybe make up for mum and dad. Then we can both visit Grenada and St. Lucia.

Jazz

Well, I've never left the valleys myself to go abroad. I hope I can do that with you sometime.

*[**Jazz** and **Luci** walk away singing an excerpt from **Love Glows with Coal** reprise]*

Jazz & Luci

En-er-gy is what you make me feel
Every time I see you
Then my world feels real

Love can run a fever
Don't you let it run cold
Cause love glows with coal

Tell me why my head is a fever
Why my heart' in 5 gear lever
Na na na na na na na na
Love glows with coal

Chorus
Ooo Na na na na na na na na
Ooo Na na na na na na na
Ooo Na na na na na na na na
Ooo Na na na na na na na na
Ooo Na na na na na na na na
Ooo Na na na na na na na
Ooo Na na na na na na na na
Ooo Na na na na na na na na

[Exit]

**SCENE :6

Wizzie Wizzie Chat

*Song: **Sweet Brown Sugar** reprise*
[Being sung in the background]

***Mama Dlo** at back at the La Sagesse Sugar Mill with her usual wizzie tools, copper pot etc. **Oz** in the secret room in the Tower of Big Pit with his wizzie tools, rum barrel etc. They are both on the wizzie web palms, checking the value of their coal and sugar investments on the stock market. Taking stock of the past, and setting the scene for the future.*

*Enter **Oz***
*[Carrying **Warner's** old sugar cane stick, laughing]*

Oz

Sometimes it takes one's own stick to break one's back. *[Laughing]*

Suggestions on Characters, Text, Songs & Language.

*****Props and settings** [Scene 7] Set on the grounds outside of Cardiff Castle. There is a special area allocated for the ponies and donkeys attending the wedding reception.*

Tell me stick, what other secrets do you hold for an old wizard like me?
[Waits for a reply]
Thank goodness you can't talk.

Mama Dlo
Oz, you silly old stick! You have the sweetest mouth in the business. You could charm the hills and the slag heaps.

Oz
It takes one to know one.

Mama Dlo
And it takes two to tango.

Oz
It's been a few years, comrade. Did you enjoy meeting the youngsters at Common Threads Internet Café last time we met?

Mama Dlo
Hallelujah! Never saw anything more hopeful than that day. Our toils and aspirations have given birth to the new generation of progress. It shows there's a lot more to be done with natural energy.

Oz
Speaking of energy, how's Trotter doing?

Mama Dlo
[Laughing]
Just imagine, Trotter had a son, Bray, and he's just like his father, he gallops along with his ears to the ground for ***nouvelle***. You know how Trotter's ears big! His big too. How's my Hoof's offspring? You know, one of them took me for a really pleasant ride around the Welsh tourist attractions when I was there last.

Oz
Grazer is his name. He's is in good fettle, my love. Tell me Mama Dlo, under what guise should I attend your Goddaughter's wedding to my good friend Devine's son? This is more than promising; I hope it won't be long before these flowers pollinate.
[Laughing]

Oz
Coal, coal, coal.

Mama Dlo
Sugar, sugar, sugar.

Oz
Warmer, warmer, warmer!

Mama Dlo
Water stand up.

Oz
Water lie down.

Mama Dlo
Time to swivel the ladle.
*[**Mama Dlo**, using her ladle, begins to stir her copper pot as well]*

Oz
Time to swivel the stick.
*[**Oz**, with his Wizzie wizzie web palm connector hand, over a crystal ball watching a marriage scene while stirring his barrel with his stick]*

*Song: **Wizzie Wizzie Wizzie** reprise*
*[Sung by **Oz** and **Mama Dlo**]*

CHORUS 1

Do the wizzie wizzie wizzie brew
Do the wizzie wizzie wizzie stew
Wizzie wizzie wizzie
Wizzie wizzie wizzie
Wizzie wizzie, wizzie wizzie
Wizzie wizzie wizzie
Brew brew wizzie wizzie brew
Stew stew wizzie wizzie stew

***Below**: The sumptuous and lavish hall for the wedding ceremony of Jazz and Luci at Cardiff Castle*

Do the Wizzie wizzie wizzie
wizzie wizzie wizzie
Wizzie wizzie wizzie wizzie
wizzie wizzie wizzie

It's a tale of mystery
Web palms history
Do the wizzie wizzie wizzie brew
Do the wizzie wizzie wizzie stew
Coal and rum A yarn of myth
Wizzie wizzie wit No hit and miss
Water stand up Water lie down
What goes up surely must
come down

CHORUS 2

Wizzie Wizzie brew
Wizzie Wizzie stew
Wizzie
Wizzie wizzie wizzie wizzie brew

No you do dis and I do dat
No Tit for tat butter for fat
Just justice
No you do dis and I do dat
No Tit for tat butter for fat
Just justice

CHORUS 2

Wizzie Wizzie brew
Wizzie Wizzie stew
Wizzie
Wizzie wizzie wizzie wizzie brew

Do the wizzie wizzie wizzie brew
Do the wizzie wizzie wizzie stew
Wizzie wizzie wizzie
Wizzie wizzie wizzie
Wizzie wizzie, wizzie wizzie
Wizzie wizzie wizzie

Oz & Mama Dlo
Bubble bubble stew stew.

Oz
What's in the stew? Something spicey?
I'll call mine Luci.

Mama Dlo
Luci, Luci! She's a touch of beauty.
We'll make her dance the
wedding romance.

Mama Dlo
Sparkle, sparkle.

Oz
Crackle, crackle.
[Marriage scene in the crystal ball ends]

Oz
Cric Crackle, Crac Crackle
Crackle Crickle, Crackle Crackle

Mama Dlo
Cric Crackle, Sparks Sparkle
Crackle Crackle, Sparkle, Sparkle

Oz
Wizzie, wizzie, wizzie

Mama Dlo
Breeze, breeze, breeze

**SCENE :7

The Wedding Reception

*Scene: **Bray** & **Grazer** are appropriately adorned in their Kingly regalia and national heraldry. They are the masters of ceremony. A long table with the cake in the middle and respective family members on lavishly decorated tables surrounding the couple.*

Grazer
Clarior E-Tenebris, brighter out of darkness. And speaking of darkness, look at Devine and Phyllis over there. I wonder if they'll be able to make up and make a go of it?

*[****Devine** and **Phyllis** talking quietly]*

Devine

Well, Phyllis my dear, you think
we could start all over again?

Phyllis

Boy, you never know. Only time will tell.

Bray

Let the light shine. We have moved from the **kerosene lamp**, extinguished the **masanto,** the lantern and the candle to switch into electricity. We movin' man, we movin'. Next to come is ethanol. All you ain't hear what the calypsonian say since the 1950s, "Go back to Coal". Seems the way crude oil is going now, we may have to look toward renewables or coal again.

***Bray**

Here's to your future.

***Grazer**

*[To **Jazz** and **Luci**]*
Cheers to your new beginning. Remember, love glows with coal and may the fruits of your knowledge bring you plenty.

Bray

Let us salute those whose toils and aspirations gave us the will to fight for freedom for all. We are all heroes and sheroes in life's struggle. Respect, I say, nuff respect.

Grazer

The grim and hungry days have left behind wounded heroes and crippled bodies, fighting to breathe, eager to live.

[They kick their feet back as if to throw stones behind their backs]

Bray

They say whey horse reach donkey must reach – Reach for your goal!

Grazer

Like the pit pony eager to see the light, so we must aspire towards the glory for our children's future. Make the young ones a beacon of hope. Let them shine.

*Music: **CT stroll** reprise*

***Luci** and **Jazz** take to the dance floor followed by the other guests.*

*Enter **Spirits of Trotter** & **Hoof***

****Spirits of Trotter & Hoof**

Guidance, Guidance.

*[Enter the rest of the cast while the spirits of **Trotter** and **Hoof** recount the **'Psalm of the Valley** below]*

Hoof

To the energies of coal, its miners and the emptied wombs who gave birth to this unending glow.

Trotter

**You gave us light. Give us hope
for peace.
Guide us through the darkness.
To the hills, though silently you
listen and look on.**

Trotter and Hoof

You'll remain the eyes, ears and manuscripts. You are the legacy of hope, the Psalm for change.

Grazer

*[Looking at **Bray**]* King Sugar!

Bray

King Coal *[Looking at **Grazer**]*

Suggestions on Characters, Text, Songs & Language.

***(Line 1 col 1) Spotlight can briefly fall on the pair in the corner, talking animatedly. **Love Glows with Coal Instrumental** or **Sweet Brown Sugar** plays in the background*

**Bray & Grazer dressed in royal regalia as King Sugar and King Coal.*

***Spirits of Trotter and Hoof (Line 18 col 2) Appear in silhouette [as if they are back from the dead].*

*(Line 22, 33, col 3 and Line 5 col 4) ***Ooe Ooe** etc the words in this refrain are similar in sound to "Oi" but pronounced in a softer, cooing fashion.*

Below:
King Sugar

Trotter
Wire ben'.

Hoof
Wizzie end.

[Revelry and dance in the style of a carnival-calypso road march]

*Song: **King Sugar King Coal***

CHORUS

Sugar Sugar, Coal Coal,
King Sugar, King Coal
Sugar Sugar, Coal Coal,
King Sugar, King Coal

Some like it hot, Some like it cold
Some like it hot, Some like it cold
King Sugar, King Coal

***Ooe, Ooe, Ooe, Ooe,**
Ooe, Ooe, Ooe, Ooe
[Whistles and percussion]

Fire Burning, Wheel turning
Wheel Turning, Fire burning
Sugar Sugar, Coal Coal,
King Sugar, King Coal
Sugar Sugar, Coal Coal,
King Sugar, King Coal

***Ooe, Ooe, Ooe, Ooe,**
Ooe, Ooe, Ooe, Ooe
[Whistles and percussion]

King Sugar, King Coal
King Sugar, King Coal
Sugar Sugar, Coal Coal,
King Sugar, King Coal

Ooe, Ooe, Ooe, Ooe
King Sugar, King Coal
Sugar Sugar, Coal Coal,
King Sugar, King Coal

Some like it hot, Some like it cold
Some like it hot, Some like it cold
King Sugar, King Coal

***Ooe, Ooe, Ooe, Ooe,**
Ooe, Ooe, Ooe, Ooe
[Whistles and percussion]

Fire Burning, Wheel turning
Wheel Turning, Fire burning
Sugar Sugar, Coal Coal,
King Sugar, King Coal
Sugar Sugar, Coal Coal,
King Sugar, King Coal

King Sugar, King Coal
King Sugar, King Coal
Sugar Sugar, Coal Coal,
King Sugar, King Coal

***Finale**: A choreographed dance celebration that leads into the audience and back to the stage before the final curtain call, featuring the principal cast members with **King Sugar** and **King Coal**, past and present, on their respective thrones.*

End

notes

Below:
King Coal

COMMON THREADS

An insight into the musical drama
Common Threads, the musical drama, where two worlds and energies collide; sugar and coal; a brew of songs and poetry. This dramatic fusion tells it all.

I became aware of the activities and the processes of the sugar cane industry as I grew up within that environment. When I first visited South Wales in the mid 1970s, the hills spoke to me, and from then onwards, I began to measure the geographic and economic similarities between Grenada and Wales. Further research led me to gain a deeper appreciation of the cultural, social and historical links between the sugar and the coal industries, which we have threaded into the script of the musical drama and the songs.

"Music reacted to the social and technological upheavals of the twentieth century as crystal does to a blow from a sledge hammer. The fragments which flew in all directions have never been adequately pieced together. Serialism, neo-classicism, socialist realism, graphical and aleatory techniques, nationalism and jazz all developed separately, only in a few cases drawing inspiration from each other. It is difficult to find one man who represents these years, but Duke Ellington... may have had as much influence as anyone on the troubled shape of music."

The above quote is from the book, ***"The Music Makers"***,[1] written in relation to Duke Ellington's contribution to the world of music, encapsulates the intentions of Common Threads: ***to draw on the multi-national milieu of peoples and music in the Caribbean and Wales that has developed throughout the centuries***.

Common threads the drama will help students to develop critical thinking and creative expression. Teachers can choose passages to help make the reading and theatrical process an enjoyable and purposeful experience.

Alex Pascall

Below:
Steel pan – The only acoustic instrument invented during the twentieth century.

Origin:
Trinidad, West Indies

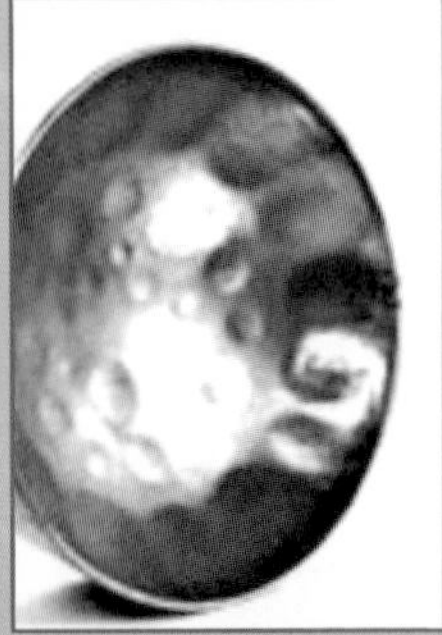

---

*Footnote: [1] **The Music Makers**, Edited by Clive Unger-Hamilton. Harrow House Editions, 1979, p221.*

A

All ah we: All of us; all you; you all

Always in we tail: Constantly bothering me

All you ease up nah: Relax

Ah sure: I'm sure

Alé Alé: ***(French Creole);*** Go, go; Move on

Amoebic guise: Always changing

A mouth champion: Someone who talks a great deal; over exaggerating

A real man pattern: To be deemed lesser than a man of stature

B

Babbledogs: Expressing anger; low worth ***(CT Language)***

Bacchanal: Very noisy merry making; noisy fun going to have a fete; big as carnival

Bagasse: Baga; *(French Creole)* The remains from sugar cane after the juice has been extracted. Often it is used as fuel to assist the making of sugar cane products. It is also used as a fertilizer

Bassodie: To be giddy; to feel light headed; confused

Bawl: Crying out loudly

Belly: *(colloquial)* see **Tummy;**

Blood thicker than water, but his thin with rum; Reference to Mr Warner's excessive drinking of alcohol, which is absorbed in the stomach and into his blood stream, hence the so called weakening, or thinning of the blood

Big Pit Colliery: One of the largest collieries in South Wales

Book-a-dull: A schemer

Bon je seye: [BON DAYE SENYE]; ***(French Creole)*** My goodness what's going on?

Bonus: Extra payment

Bosh: A wash basin or kitchen sink ***(S.Wales dialect)*** German derivative

Bull pistle: (East. Caribbean); cow-cod* Could be used as an instrument for discipline. *Also a culinary delicacy, hence cow-cod soup

Black lung: [PNEUMONICONSIS] A medical condition coal miners suffer from. Caused by inhalation of fine coal dust. see ***Pneumoniconsis***

C

Calabash: The brown dried, football sized gourd of the calabash tree. When cut into two and used as a utensil.

Café con Léche: Coffee with milk

Carenage: The area surrounding the harbour

Caribs: Carib women; Some of the indigenous people of the Caribbean Islands; Tuki, the last of the Carib women to leap into the sea.

Cawl, ***(Welsh);*** A German derived word a broth, very nutritious on a cold winters day

Ceridwen: ***(Welsh);*** Witch

Clarior E-Tenebris: ***(Latin);*** meaning 'brighter out of darkness'; let the light shine

CO_2: Carbondioxide

Coal-pot fire: A coal-stove, a small round cast-iron charcoal burning open stove used for cooking and roasting.

Coal pits: ***(Caribbean, African);*** A small hole dug into the ground and filled with logs of wood, then covered with bushes and earth and set alight to burn slowly to produce charcoal

Cold liquor: The juice extracted from crushing the sugar cane

Cocoa tea: Hot beverage made from the cocoa bean

Cockroach in front frizzle fowl: An easy prey

Conch shell: The empty shell of the conch, a shell fish used like a horn, acts as a warning signal when blown. (***The conch shell represents the original name of the island of Grenada, Camahogne***)

Congotay: To get your just deserts

Cool it: Don't upset things

Coo Coo Soup: [KOU KOU] ***(French Creole)***; A meal made from grinding maize (corn) with other ingredients. However, when someone says they will make you a ***"Coo Coo soup"***, it means that they wish to do you some harm, you ought to be warned

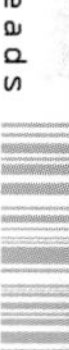

Corpse-candles: Lanterns in Welsh windows signifying that someone is about to die

Crab mentality: Keeping someone at the bottom of the barrel; stop one bettering themselves

Cramping me style: You upsetting my plans; stopping progress

Crapaud: Crapo; [KWAPO] ***(French Creole);*** A frog

Crapo smoke he pipe: To be in real trouble; things are in a bad way

Crayfish: A small river fish from the shrimp family, a delicacy used in cooking

Crépe en flambé: [KWÉP EN FLAMBÉ] A dessert similar to a pancake, doused in rum which is then set alight ***(en flambé)*** to release the flavour

Cribo: A snake, dark brown in colour, with a thick neck. A powerful constrictor, it can grow to 7ft in length; present in Caribbean mythology

Cric-crac: Call and response; In the structure of storytelling

Croeso: [CROY-SO] ***(Welsh);*** Welcome

Crop - over: A festival, celebrating the harvesting of the sugar cane

Cunumunu: ***Ku-nu mu-nu***; [COO NU MOO NU] ***(French Creole);*** A stupid person

Cut style: To show off

Cutting on both sides: Someone who pretends not to take sides; somewhat of a hypocrite

D

Dafydd: ***(Welsh);*** David

Davey lamp: A type of lamp used by miners

Dem: Them

Dirty water: Superstitious belief that when one dreams about dirty water, trouble is sure to follow

Done talk: That's it! finished

Donkey Street: A street in Wales named after an area where many donkeys were found. Donkeys were used to transport coal

Doom, Doom,: Common threads drum

Dotish: Senseless

Dracula: A Vampire who is reputed to suck his victim's blood

Dumplin': Dough. A delicacy of the Caribbean made with flour, water and salt. A pot of soup without dumplings would not be complete.

Dumplins: Same as dumpling, made from flour and water

E

Ease up nah: Stop harassing me

Eh eh: An utterance when someone is surprised

Eisteddfod: ***(Welsh);*** The local festival held in each of the valley communities as well as district and national events; Part of the popular entertainment festival, Eisteddfod

Emoticons: Symbols and text language shortcuts used when emailing via the internet or text messaging

Engine Rowe: Housing originally built for key workers

Ethanol: A colourless liquid produced from petroleum gas, used to make soap, a cleansing agent.

F

Farine: Maze or cassava; ***(Amerindian);*** A starchy root vegetable; Coarse grain meal made from the grated residue of bitter cassava (after squeezing out the poisonous juice); Farine is used in a number of ways, as a cereal, thickening gravy, making dumplings

Fe he mischief: To hide his evil doings

Flambeau: ***(French);*** **Flambo;** ***(French Creole)*** A bottle filled with kerosene or oil with flammable material as a stopper then lit to light your way walking in the dark

Full up ah things and things: Everything and nothing at the same time

'Fraid: To be afraid

Frankenstein: A man like monster who inherited the name of his creator, Victor Frankenstein

G

GBSS: Grenada Boys Secondary School, the

oldest grammar school in Grenada.

Give a goat an inch of slack it goin' take a foot!: The more one gets, the more one wants. To take advantage of privileges given

Glyn: *(Welsh);* Glen

GMMWU: Grenada Manual and Mental Workers Union

Grand Étang Forest: A rainforest of Grenada which encompasses the Grand Étang lake, an old volcanic crater

Grabble Phantoms: A group of hidden enemies *(CT language)*

Guava cheese: A confectionery made from the guava fruit, with sugar, spices and other ingredients

Grinding stone: Used for sharpening tools made of steel

H

Headgear: The tower of the mining colliery

Hear de tune: Listen to the tune

Hear nah: Listen to this

He don't lose he tail: He does not get hurt

He who pays the piper calls the tune: The person paying the wages dictates the terms

Hibiscus: A brightly coloured tropical flower

Hic incipt incantamentum: Here beginneth the spell

Hound of the Baskervilles: A classic tale, written by Sir Arthur Conan Doyle

I

If all wishes were horses all beggars would ride: Imagining the impossible

Iguana: A large tropical lizard

Iguana man: [ARAWAK]; Camouflaged; a disguise; in order to conceal one's personality

It's action in he tail: Now the action begins; blow by blow

I done see: I've already seen

I goin' miss this man bad: To miss a friend's presence deeply

J

Jab Jab: (From the french ***Diable)*** - meaning devil in disguise

Jackass: A donkey

Jack o' lantern: A lantern made from a hollowed out pumpkin. Holes are cut to represent facial features

Jalousie: *(French);* A wooden louvered blind.

Jumbie: The ghost of the dead, human or animal. the term linking good or evil with the same cosmic power, a spirit like character used to induce fear

Just baiting for you: Waiting in anticipation to catch someone out; unsuspecting

Just sit tight: Sit still; relax

K

Ketch: To catch; take hold of

Kerosene lamp: A lamp made locally, home made that uses kerosene oil to light the darkness

L

Ladle: A wooden pot spoon

La Sagesse: Sugar cane plantation in Grenada situated in the parish of St David's

Ladjablès: *(French Creole);* A mythical character in Caribbean folklore. A beautiful woman always dressed in white with one human foot and one cow foot. She is able to beguile men with her beauty and lead them to their uncertain end

Le Mon de Sauteurs: Leapers Hill, the place where the last of the Caribs jumped into the sea to avoid capture by the French invaders of the Island Grenada

Leek soup: *(Welsh);* A traditional welsh soup made from the leek plant

Leh we go: Let us go; *(used in narrative dialogue)*

Like an Iguana: In the play the term is used to describe Warner as a shady character, someone you can't trust, or changes his mind often. see ***Iguana man***

Lime: Laze about, to hang about socially

Listen to we: Listen to us

Look sharp: To be smartly dressed

Look him deh: Look at him over there

Long rope for maga goat: *(French Creole);* Give someone enough rope, they'll hang themselves, without anybody's help given time

Lose he tail: To get a good beating

M

Maga: *(French Creole) Meagré;* Thin, slim person;

Mamaguy: Skillful flatter; teasing or deception often in a lighthearted manner

Mama Dlo: A mythical goddess, in Caribbean folklore, goddess of the water, she inhabits lakes, and rivers.

Manicou: A rodent closely related to the possum

Manicou man: A term used here to highlight the character of Mr Warner likened to a rodent, unscrupulous and selfish

Market Hill: A famous steep hill in the town of St Georges in Grenada.

Masanto: see ***Flambeau***

Masquerader: Usually recognised in a disguise in merry making, carnival

Mèsi: Thank you

Misyé: *(French Creole);* Mr, Mister

Miner's Union: Confederation of individuals for a common purpose eg. better working conditions;

Molasses: Thick dark syrup drained from fermenting sugar cane juice in the refining process

Mongoose men: A term used to describe a hand picked group of henchmen that carries out acts of brutality at the orders of a leader or someone with power. Men so employed are popularly named Mongoose gang

Monkey say cool breeze, crapaud say, wait until tomorrow: It's your turn today, but you had better watch out, it could be mine tomorrow

Monologue: Dramatic piece for one performer; long speech by one person

Mouth champion: Having a lot to say

Mountain Dove: Ground dove, mourning dove

Muckers: The workers who remove waste from mines or stables

Mulching: Decaying leaves, compost, spread around plants to enrich the soil

N

Nah: No

Nation Dance: African nation dance, one of a number of dances identified with the heritage of a particular tribe.

Non Palma sin Labore: No reward without labour

Nouvelle: *(French Creole);* Give me the news

Nutmeg: A spice; the fruit from the nutmeg tree

O

Oil Down: National dish of Grenada; the process of boiling down the vegetable and meat e.g., pork, the oil resulting from the use of coconut milk

One for the road: To have a drink before leaving to take to the road on the way home

P

Palimpsest: A parchment or other writing material written upon twice, the original writing having been erased or rubbed out to make place for the second; a manuscript in which a later writing is written over an erased earlier writing

Pappy Show: A thing, a situation, proceeding or an event that is ridiculous or embarrassing

Paul Robeson: Famous black American singer, scholar and civil rights activists

Picket line: A person or group standing outside the work place to deter workers from entering the building or grounds. Used when trade unionists take industrial action and withdraw their labour (strike), in order to achieve better pay, or working conditions. A person who crosses this line to go to work is known as a scab see ***Scab***

Penny wise and pound foolish: To gain less in the end, a bad decision

Pneumoconiosis: see ***'Black lung'***

Primus stove: Portable cooking stove that burns vapourised oil

R

Ram packed: Tightly packed

Read he upside down, Could tell what you are up to

Real licks: Heavy punishment

Rice tea: Made from rice with spices and milk, or coconut milk, a porridge

Roasted corn: Maize, corn on the cob roasted on charcoal fire

Rook pie: ***(Welsh);*** A pie made from a young rook, a bird similar to the raven; A popular country dish

Rum: Alcohol processed from the sugar cane juice

Rum Casket: Container/barrel for rum

Rum shop jumbie: Description of a person addicted to alcohol who frequents the rum shop Jumbie; spirit like character

Rush de brush, you'll get daub: If you look for trouble you'll get it

S

Saffron: A root spice with a deep yellow colour, shaped like a ginger root

Sauteurs: ***(French Creole);*** The name of a small town in Grenada

Scabs: Someone who breaks a picket line see ***picket line***

Scratching Zutie and smelling about: Stop wasting time ***(Grenada)***

Shango: A traditional African religious ceremony; a cultural custom of the Yoruba tribe, offerings and prayers are made to the gods. In the text, the prayers are asking for rain to replenish the crops.

She who holds the iron knows the heat: She who holds the purse string is in command

Ship sail, sail fast!: How many men on board a riddle used for a guessing game; Popularly played in Grenada at that time, with shelled roasted corn to guess how many seeds of corn are held in the hand

Show me your motions: To dance for admiration

Shu fly, don't bother me: Leave me alone

Sky Red! A term brought about by the burning of plantation and agricultural lands by strikers in the workers' revolt for better pay and working conditions in the General strike in Grenada

Souse: Delicacy made from pig trotters

Spice things up: Liven up situations

Stew peas: Pigeon peas cooked in a particular way, popular in the Caribbean

Still water does run deep: One cannot trust quiet people

St Josephs Convent: Convent school in Grenada

Steups: Sucking ones teeth, depending on when it is used it can mean different things, ie dismissing someone in annoyance

Stupidie: Not sensible; see ***Cunumunu***

Sugarcake: Grated coconut, boiled in a mixture of sugar, coconut milk spices, essence, laid out in small amounts like little cakes

Su Su: ***(French Creole);*** A weekly or monthly contribution made by each participant; A way of saving money, to receive the total sum when it is your turn. Mostly used in the Southern Caribbean; It is called ***'Partner'*** in Jamaica, for the benefit of Jamaican children/pupils

The **Su su bank:** see ***Su su***

Sweet food kill cow: Greediness can be your downfall

Sweet potatoes: Vegetable, an edible tuber with purple, pinkish or cream thin skin

T

Teach she: Teach her

Tenor steel pan: A musical instrument made from the oil drum. Originates from Trinidad. The lead instrument in an orchestra of steel pans which carries the melody

That iguana man: see ***Iguana***

The only rooster in the yard: Believing that no one else is as important or as powerful as himself ***(reference to Mr Warner)***

To boot!: Well! fancy that

Too fresh up: Too pushy, too bossy

Trouble trouble, trouble bound to trouble you: If you interfere with anyone you must take the consequences

Tummy: A part of the body containing the stomach and intestines

U

see ***Miner's Union***

V

Valley Inheritance Museum: The main museum that deals with the history of coal mining

W

Wait na!: Wait

Wake: A prayer meeting held during the period of mourning a death in the family

Water stand up,Water lie down: It is a riddle ***"water stand up water lie down",*** the answer to the riddle is sugar cane ie because the sugar cane is practically water in content,whether it is lying or standing

Wavet pa ni wezon douvan poul: The cockroach you want to catch is parading again

Web palm: A Wizzie wizzie world of the Invisible (WWWI) palm device, a tool that allows wizzie comrades to communicate. It is recessed in the palm of the hand, and powered by the energy of the body. It glows brightly when in use

We donkey: Our donkey

We way: Our way

West Indian Islands: The name given to the Caribbean Islands by christopher Columbus

Wet our whistle: To have a drink of alcohol, in this case, rum

What goes up, must come down: Whatever one does, expect the same in return

What nice from far is far from nice: Things are not what they seem

What ain't pass you don't say it miss you: Your turn is sure to come, do not think you have escaped

What sweet in goats mouth goes sour in its tail: What seems good will eventually become quite unpleasant

Where horse reach, donkey must reach: Here, the term is used to mean, one can achieve anything

Whey: Where;

Who the cap fit, let them wear it: A common saying, like it or not, if you are the guilty one you should bear the consequences

Why pour oil on troubled waters: Don't make things worse than they already are

WIBS: ***Windward Islands Broadcasting Service*** The radio station was located in Grenada in the fifties to broadcast to the neighbouring Islands of the Southern Caribbean

Will-o'- the wisp: Bent light rays sometimes seen over marshes at night; An illusive person

Wizzie wizzie wizzie: A concoction mixed by the wizards and sorceress to cure, frighten or to be given as punishment

wwwpc: Wizzie Wizzie Web palm connector

Wizzie Wizzie World of the Invisible: ***(WWWI)*** The land of wizards and sorcerers. Also a retreat where humans, such as Mr Warner, can be exiled to. For rehabilitation of whatever ails them. They are met by superhumans of the Ancient World, such as Oz Mosis, Mama Dlo, Asteroditis, Kinetisis, Saccharoditus, and super animals that will assist during the rehabilitation period ***(see p16)***

Y

Yams: A root vegetable rich in starch. It is highly cultivated in Africa ***(especially in Ghana)*** and throughout the Caribbean Islands

York House: Government building in Grenada where the Island's Parliament is held

You ain't hear: Did you hear, take notice?

You like cow and no respect for its calf: Lacking respect for one's close relatives

Z

Zouk: ***(French Creole);*** Communal dance, the music with brass instruments, drums, electric guitar and keyboards, singers and costumed dancers. The music is vigorously rhythmic, four crochets to the bar with brass and singers dominant. It is described as the ***'rock music'*** of the tropics. All the challenging social aspects of rock can be found in Zouk.

Zutie: ***(French Creole);***
One of the most painful stinging nettles one can encounter in the sugar cane fields in Grenada

CT MUSICAL THREADS

In 1594, a group of men met regularly in Florence, Italy, because they wanted to introduce a fresh fashion in dramatic theatre, which eventually gave rise to the Opera. Much like them, Dad and I set out to make a fresh statement in musical script, for contemporary stage theatre, filmed musicals and animation.

CommonThreads characters speech delivery is variable in language, age, class, culture and time. A combination of the obvious and the less obvious with subtleties of the common threads that exist in both Caribbean and Welsh music has been explored. I used his original script and theme to fuse Caribbean, Welsh cultural musical styles and diverse language patterns with other popular music forms and instruments to tell this musical story, within that, a new dance form, ***The Stroll***, evolved.

CT Stroll like ***CT Prelude***, *(bearing the same suffix "CT" to allow for the option of a contemporary dance being performed within the Prelude)*, combines musical genres of retentive African and European origins which hark to the spirits of all who have inhabited, invaded, or settled in Grenada. ***The Stroll*** is a musical dance form written with an ambiguous metered introduction reminiscent of flamenco, calypso and reggae rhythms that overlay a swaggering melodic theme in 3/4, time to kick-start the languid "stroll", in the style of a walk. It is done with a large stride to the left, another to the right and the next to the back with the left foot. At first, with more energy and momentum thrown to the "1" instead of "2" and "3". The emphasis of the beat alternates as the form moves on, to project the hazy feeling after a night's celebration at Eisteddfod or Trinidad-like Carnival euphoria or a drunken happy state.

The intention of the instrumentals in CommonThreads is to evoke images where there is no script or to provide accompaniment. However, these are not its only functions, as each work can stand-alone in concert settings.

"Wherever communication is the key between nations - music and dance reign supreme". ***(D.P.)***

ABOUT THE AUTHOR:

Common Threads and the many sides of Alex Pascall OBE

© Charles Green (Master of Photography)

Alex Pascall was born in Grenada and educated at Grenada Boys Secondary School, the island's leading grammar school. He spent his early childhood on Hope Vale Sugar Cane Estate where his aunt and uncle were managers. A career in agriculture beckoned. But the young Pascall was smitten by the folk culture and performance arts of the Caribbean. He secured a position as a percussionist with the Bee Wee Ballet Dance Troupe and set sail for Britain with the company in July 1959 determined to pursue his goal in communication, music and culture. By night he took to the stage as a drummer/vocalist in West End clubs and restaurants with his own bands and by day he worked as a Guard/Motorman on the London Underground. Throughout the 1960s and early 1970s, Alex created and performed with an impressive variety of musical ensembles – from a ten-piece dance band, The Magnets, to a series of vocal trios and quartets specialising in popular songs of the African diaspora to the hugely successful Alex Pascall Singers, a ground-breaking choir which introduced to British audiences the diverse musical styles of the Caribbean, from kumina to calypso, from work songs to mento.

In 1974 his career took a dramatic turn when he became the presenter and producer of "Black Londoners", aired on BBC Radio London, the first daily Black radio programme in Britain. It quickly became the focal point and outlet for Black British art and culture, sport and politics. Whatever was significant for London's black communities, at home or in the Caribbean, found a voice on "Black Londoners". Alex was a natural broadcaster, and over the next fourteen years his became one of the most distinctive and recognisable voices on British radio, his deep Eastern Caribbean voice was a welcome, nightly companion in every Caribbean home and Londoners as a whole. During his tenure at the BBC, Alex's journalism blossomed. He co-founded the Voice newspaper. He became a member of the National Union of Journalists (NUJ) in 1979 and has been a member of its National Executive Council since 1998. and is also Chair of the NUJ's Black Members Council.

A long-time supporter of the Notting Hill carnival, and Founder/Vice-Chair of the Foundation for European Carnival Cities, he has also served as Chair of the Notting Hill Carnival and Arts Committee from 1984-89

From broadcasting Alex has focused his energies working with schools to enrich the learning experience of Britain's children through creativity in education projects, drama, music and storytelling. He wrote and performed some of the most memorable lullabies for the BBC's world famous Teletubbies series. For the past four years, Alex created and implemented a series of community education programmes for schools nationally, including the much acclaimed "Roots to Torfaen" project for 52 schools in the Borough of Torfaen, South Wales, which has been commended as an exemplar project by the ACCAC for Wales.

Alex Pascall was awarded the OBE for services to community relations in 1996.

NOTES ABOUT THE TYPOGRAPHY:

The typeface for this book is Gill Sans set in Gill Sans 11 on 15 pt.The typeface Gill Sans was designed by Eric Gill and released by the Monotype Corporation between 1928 and 1930, Gill Sans is based on the typeface Edward Johnston, the innovative British letterer and teacher, designed in 1916 for the signage of the London Underground.

Gill's alphabet is more classical in proportion and contains his signature flared capital **R** and eyeglass lowercase **g**. With distinct roots in pen-written letters, Gill Sans is classified as a humanist sans serif, making it very legible and readable in text and display work. The condensed, bold, and display versions are excellent for packaging or posters.

ABOUT THE TYPOGRAPHER:

Eric Gill — In 1928 Gill Sans font was designed to create a contrast font to the austerity of the geometric San Serif's fonts, which were popular at this time. The font was inspired by Edward Johnston's type for the London Underground Railroad of 1916. **Stanley Morison,** ***(The innovative British letterer and teacher)*** had seen Gill's letters on a store front sign, and urged Eric Gill to develop the letters into a typeface.

The font was released in 1929 and quickly became the most popular Sans Serif typeface in Britain.This font is thought to be Gills most significant design accomplishment.

Gill Sans is classified as a humanist face, meticulously patterned after classic Roman characters proportions.This gained it a reputation as the most legible Sans Serif design of the time. It is very similar in structure to **Perpetua**, another of Gill's most popular type design— ***(So named after one of his daughters)*** Some of the more distinctive earmarks that characterize this face are an **M** with a high pointed central function; an **R** with a curved leg; a **J** with a short tail; and a **W** and **V** with pointed bases.

Eric Gill was a sculptor and carver of Inscriptional lettering. He was also a wood carver, book illustrator, and essayist on cultural issues.

notes

Common threads

COAL MINERS BALLA

'NEATH V
WITH MAND

OUT TWELVE HOUR SHIFTS
'NEATH VALLEYS FO
WITH MANDRILL AND SH
EAT WITH GAS RISING, RE TR
OPLE TRUCKING PONIES W
GOTTA STEP ON TH
EAT
IT'S HARD BREATHING
WHEELS A TURNING
TO M SKIDS ON TUP
'NEATH VALL
WITH MANDRILL AND
LAMP KIT IN THE HEAT
PEOPLE TRUCK
DEAD BEAT!
GOTTA STE
BEFORE
BREATHING, WANNA L

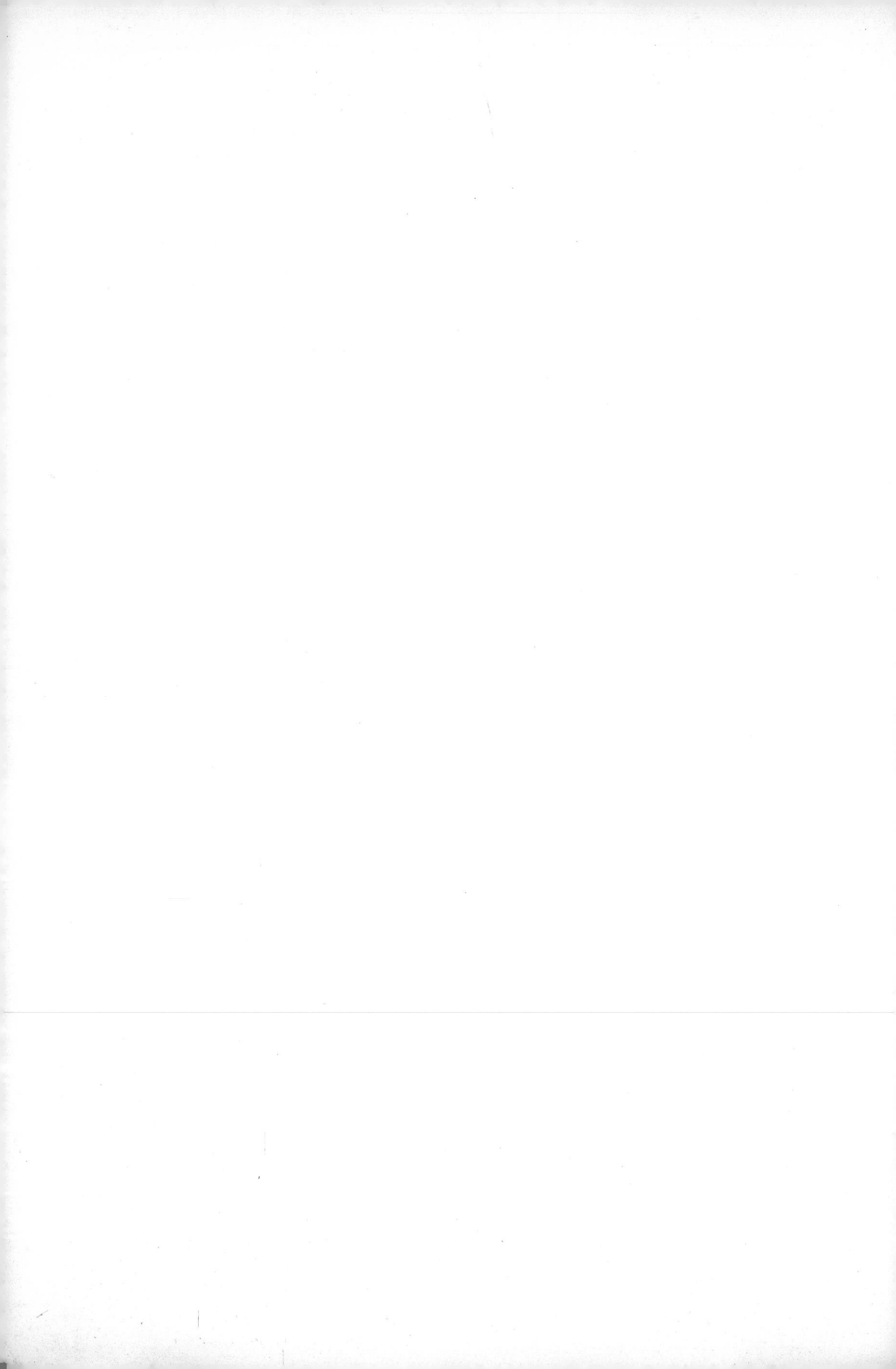